Trash TO TREASURE

Before you throw away another milk carton or plastic soda bottle, take a look at Trash to Treasure! Then start sorting through your wastebaskets and recycling bins, because you're on the path to a creative way of recycling. This all-new volume of imaginative projects is your road map to transforming seemingly useless throwaways into works of art. Our fun-filled book features four sections, each jam-packed with fresh ways to fix up old discards. Make your way through Holiday Magic to celebrate those special times of the year, and browse through Great Gifts for presents "renewed" with your handmade touch. Home Sweet Spruce-Ups will help you add spice to that place you call home, while Fun Fix-Ups has projects for folks of all ages to enjoy. Using empty detergent boxes, fabric scraps, old silverware, food containers, and your own two hands, you can create over 125 projects while saving money — and helping to clean up our planet! With easy-to-follow instructions and full-color photographs to help you chart your course, you'll want to make them all. So what are you waiting for? Let's get started on your journey down the trail of clever "recycling!"

Anne Childs

LEISURE ARTS, INC.
Little Rock, Arkansas

EDITORIAL STAFF

Vice President and Editor-in-Chief:
   Anne Van Wagner Childs
Executive Director: Sandra Graham Case
Design Director: Patricia Wallenfang Sowers
Editorial Director: Susan Frantz Wiles
Publications Director: Kristine Anderson Mertes
Creative Art Director: Gloria Bearden
Senior Graphics Art Director: Melinda Stout

DESIGN
Designers: Katherine Prince Horton, Sandra Spotts Ritchie,
   Anne Pulliam Stocks, Linda Diehl Tiano,
   and Rebecca Sunwall Werle
Executive Assistants: Billie Steward and Debra Smith
Design Assistant: Melanie Vaughan

TECHNICAL
Managing Editor: Charlotte Loftin
Copy Editor: Barbara McClintock Vechik
Senior Technical Writer: Christopher M. McCarty
Technical Writers: Jennifer L. Hobbs and
   Laura Lee Powell
Technical Associates: Susan McManus Johnson
   and Briget Julia Laskowski

EDITORIAL
Managing Editor: Linda L. Trimble
Associate Editor: Stacey Robertson Marshall
Assistant Editors: Terri Leming Davidson
   and Janice Teipen Wojcik

ART
Book/Magazine Graphics Art Director: Diane M. Hugo
Senior Graphics Illustrator: Wendy Ward Lair
Photography Stylists: Beth Carter, Pam Choate,
   Sondra Daniel, Karen Smart Hall, Aurora Huston,
   Courtney Jones, and Laura Reed

PROMOTIONS
Managing Editors: Alan Caudle and
   Marjorie Ann Lacy
Associate Editors: Steven M. Cooper, Dixie L. Morris,
   Jennifer Ertl Wobser, Ellen Clifton, and Marie Trotter
Designer: Dale Rowett
Art Director: Linda Lovette Smart
Production Artist: Leslie Loring Krebs
Publishing Systems Administrator: Cindy Lumpkin
Publishing Systems Assistants: Susan Mary Gray and
   Rob Walker

BUSINESS STAFF

Publisher: Bruce Akin
Vice President, Marketing: Guy A. Crossley
Vice President and General Manager: Thomas L. Carlisle
Retail Sales Director: Richard Tignor
Vice President, Retail Marketing: Pam Stebbins

Retail Marketing Director: Margaret Sweetin
Retail Customer Service Manager: Carolyn Pruss
General Merchandise Manager: Cathy Laird
Vice President, Finance: Tom Siebenmorgen
Distribution Director: Rob Thieme

Library of Congress Catalog Number 98-65089
International Standard Book Number 1-57486-078-X

TABLE OF CONTENTS

Holiday MAGIC 6

Great GIFTS 38

TABLE OF CONTENTS

Home Sweet SPRUCE-UPS......................70

TABLE OF CONTENTS

Holiday MAGIC

*M*ake your holiday celebrations especially festive by creating fun, resourceful projects using items that would ordinarily be thrown away! You'll find a bundle of crafty ways to fashion unique gifts and quick decorations for your home while you help to save our planet. Create treasures such as Valentine sun catchers from plastic food containers, delicate Easter candles using eggshells, a "batty" Halloween wreath out of bubble wrap, or old-fashioned Christmas stockings, like the ones shown here, using odd socks. No matter what your traditions are, you're sure to discover some clever new ones in the pages of Holiday Magic.

Valentine Sun Catchers

Pretty pastels and scallop-trimmed heart designs make our Valentine sun catchers an elegant way to adorn windows during the most romantic month of the year. Created with dimensional and acrylic paints, the window valentines are fashioned from clear plastic food containers backed with tissue paper. A string of crystal beads provides a delicate hanger for each one.

Valentine Sun Catchers

Recycled item: clear plastic food containers.

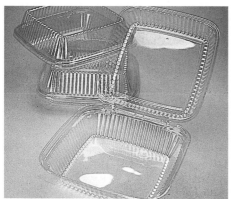

You will also need: black permanent medium-point marker, white tissue paper, black dimensional paint, desired colors of acrylic paint, paintbrushes, pushpin, clear thread, clear bugle beads, and craft glue.

1. For each sun catcher, cut a flat piece from plastic container. Use marker to trace desired pattern, pages 130 and 131, onto front of plastic piece.
2. Using equal parts water and glue, thin glue. Glue tissue paper to back of plastic; allow to dry.
3. Use dimensional paint to paint over lines on plastic piece; allow to dry.

4. Using equal parts water and acrylic paint, thin paint. Using dimensional paint lines as a guide, paint tissue paper; allow to dry.
5. Cut out sun catcher along outer lines of design.
6. Use pushpin to make a small hole in top of sun catcher. Insert thread through hole and string beads to desired length for hanger; knot ends.

SWEETHEART SHIRT

*S*hare hugs and kisses and lots of love with everyone you see when you wear this fanciful Valentine top. A plain white oxford shirt decorated with cute appliqués and paint makes a "love-ly" holiday statement to the romantic at heart.

VALENTINE SHIRT

Recycled items: shirt and fabric scraps. *You will also need:* tracing paper, paper-backed fusible web, compressed craft sponges, desired colors of acrylic paint, black permanent medium-point marker, black permanent fine-point marker, and replacement buttons (optional).

1. Wash and dry shirt without fabric softener.
2. Using patterns, page 133, follow *Making Appliqués,* page 157, to make desired number of heart appliqués from fabric scraps. Arranging as desired, fuse appliqués to shirt. Follow *Machine Appliqué,* page 158, to stitch around edges of appliqués.

3. For painted hearts, X's, and O's, trace desired patterns, page 133, onto tracing paper. Use patterns to cut shapes from compressed sponges. Use sponge shapes and follow *Sponge Painting,* page 159, to paint shirt. Use fine-point marker to add "stitches" around hearts and medium-point marker to add stars, swirls, and wavy lines inside painted hearts.
4. For each cuff, cut original cuff from shirt. Baste sleeve placket closed. Measure around edge of sleeve. Cut an 8"w piece of fabric 1" longer than edge of sleeve. Matching wrong sides and short edges, use a 1/2" seam allowance to sew short edges

together. Matching wrong sides and raw edges, fold cuff in half. Matching raw edges and seams, place cuff in sleeve. Use a 1/4" seam allowance to sew cuff to sleeve. Turn cuff out over sleeve and press in place. Repeat for remaining cuff.
5. To cover collar, lay shirt collar flat on tracing paper. Draw around collar on tracing paper; cut out 1/4" outside drawn lines. Use pattern to cut collar cover from desired fabric. Press all edges 1/4" to wrong side. Matching edges, baste collar cover to top of shirt collar. Topstitch along each edge of collar.
6. If desired, replace buttons.

The Easter bunny has found his way into your holiday egg hunt to help collect an armload of colorful eggs! Our cute bunny basket features a stuffed sock head with big, floppy ears and feet. His outstretched arms hold a painted basket with plenty of room for treats and hard-boiled treasures.

Recycled items: basket (we used a 5" x 9¼" oval basket), one white terry-lined adult tube sock, and a fabric scrap for inner ears.

You will also need: desired color spray paint for basket, tracing paper, transfer paper, polyester fiberfill, 8" x 10" piece of white felt, pink felt for nose and cheeks, black embroidery floss, six 2" pieces of white cloth-covered wire, two ¼" dia. black buttons for eyes, 2" dia. silk daisy, 20" of ⅝"w ribbon, 2¼"w ribbon to go around basket, white poster board, black permanent fine-point marker, and a hot glue gun.

1. Spray paint basket; allow to dry.
2. Matching arrows and grey lines on bunny top and bunny arm sections, trace bunny, muzzle, foot, ear, cheek, and nose patterns, page 134, onto tracing paper; cut out.
3. Cut cuff from sock. For head and arms, draw around bunny pattern on foot section of sock. Sewing along drawn lines and leaving an opening for turning, sew through both layers of sock. Turn bunny inside out and stuff with fiberfill. Sew opening closed.
4. For muzzle, use pattern to cut one muzzle from white felt. Stitching ⅛" inside edge, work *Running Stitch,* page 159, around muzzle piece. Stuff muzzle lightly with fiberfill while pulling threads to loosely gather muzzle; knot thread to secure. For whiskers, glue wire pieces to wrong side of muzzle. Glue muzzle to head.
5. For feet, use foot pattern to cut two feet from sock cuff and two from white felt. Leaving an opening for stuffing, use a ¼" seam allowance to sew one cuff piece to one felt piece. Turn inside out and stuff. Sew openings closed. Use floss to stitch details on feet and paws.
6. Use cheek and nose patterns to cut two cheeks and one nose from pink felt. Glue cheeks and nose to muzzle. Sew buttons to face for eyes. Use floss to work *Straight Stitch*, page 159, for mouth and a stitch from nose to mouth.
7. For ears, use pattern to cut two ears from white felt. Draw around pattern twice on fabric scrap; cut out inner ears ⅛" inside drawn line. Glue one inner ear to each felt ear. Making a ¼" pleat in bottom edge of each ear, glue ears to back of head. Glue daisy to one ear.
8. Glue bunny along top back edge of basket. Glue feet to top front edge of basket. Tie ⅝"w ribbon into a bow around bunny's neck.
9. Overlapping ribbon ends at back, glue 2¼"w ribbon around basket.
10. Trace banner design, page 135, onto tracing paper. Use transfer paper to transfer design to poster board; cut out along outside lines. Use marker to write message and draw "stitches" around banner. Glue banner to front of basket.

EGGSHELL CANDLES

*M*uch too pretty to be hidden, our Easter eggs make delightful decorative candles! You might find similar styles in expensive specialty stores, but it's easy (and inexpensive) to make your own using empty eggshells as wax molds. After the wax hardens, the shells are removed and simple painted patterns are added.

EGG CANDLES

Recycled items: eggshells, egg carton, can for melting wax, and newspaper to protect work surface.

You will also need: bleach, rubber gloves, cooking spray, candle wax or paraffin, pan to hold can while melting wax, wax-coated wicks, small paintbrush, and desired colors of acrylic paint.

1. (*Caution:* Wear rubber gloves and work in a well-ventilated area when working with bleach.) For each candle, make a dime-size hole in narrow end of egg; drain egg. Rinse shell with water, then with bleach. Allow to dry completely.

2. Lightly spray inside of shell with cooking spray. Stand shell upright in egg carton.

3. Follow *Working with Wax*, page 158, to melt wax. Fill shell ¾ full with wax. Allow wax to harden slightly; insert wick. Allow wax to cool.

4. Remove shell from candle. Paint candle as desired; allow to dry.

"EGG-CITING" EASTER BOUQUET

*B*righten a too-quiet table this Easter with this vivid bouquet of painted paper flowers. Arranged in a fabric-covered potato chip canister, these blooms started out as the bottom of an egg carton. Add splashes of paint and button centers, and you can have the feeling of spring all year round!

EGG CARTON BOUQUET

Recycled items: paper egg carton (one carton will make five flowers), 3/4" dia. buttons for flower centers, and a snack chip container for vase.

For each flower, you will also need: foam brushes, sponge pieces, two colors of acrylic paint (for base color and highlight color), paper towels, pushpin, 20" of floral wire, green floral tape, tracing paper, 2" square of green felt, and a hot glue gun.
For vase, you will also need: fabric, 28" of 1½"w wired ribbon, artificial flowers and greenery for filler, and spray adhesive.

1. For each flower, cut petal piece from center section of egg carton (Fig. 1).

Fig. 1

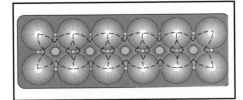

2. Paint petal piece with base color; allow to dry. Follow *Sponge Painting*, page 159, to lightly paint highlight color onto petal piece; allow to dry.
3. Trace calyx pattern, page 130, onto tracing paper. Use pattern to cut calyx from felt. Hot glue calyx to bottom of petal piece.
4. Use pushpin to punch two holes through center of petal piece and calyx. Bend wire in half and thread through button holes and flower. Twist wire together at bottom of flower; wrap wire with floral tape.
5. For vase, measure around container; add ½". Measure height of container. Cut a piece of fabric the determined measurements. Apply spray adhesive to wrong side of fabric piece; glue fabric around container.
6. Tie ribbon into a bow around vase.
7. Arrange flowers and filler in vase.

13

SPIRITED UNCLE SAM

Everyone will get a bang out of our flag-toting friend! Outfitted in stars and stripes, this spirited greeter is easily made from cardboard gift wrap tubes covered with patriotic fabrics. He's truly a fitting tribute to the fabulous Fourth!

UNCLE SAM

Recycled items: 30" length of 3¼" dia. cardboard tube for body, two 6¾" lengths of 1¼" dia. cardboard tube for arms, poster board, sand to weight body, two ½" dia. black buttons for eyes, two ¾" dia. black buttons for shoes, one ¾" dia. and two ½" dia. red buttons for shirt and cuffs.

You will also need: tracing paper; compass; craft knife; craft stick for nose; flesh, yellow, and black acrylic paint; paintbrushes; one 4"w and three 1½"w wooden stars; one 4"w and one 5½"w wooden heart; striped fabric cut into one 10½" x 10½" piece for pants and one 5¾" x 10½" piece for hat; star-print fabric cut into one 10½" x 10½" piece for shirt, two 4½" x 6¾" pieces for arms, and two 8" x 10" pieces; 5" x 10½" piece of flesh-color fabric for face; 10½" of 1"w ribbon for hat trim; plastic sandwich bag with seal; white craft fur cut into 4" x 7" piece for hair, ½" x 3" piece for eyebrow, and 2" x 8" piece for beard; red medium-point marker; long nail; one 7½" and one 12" length of heavy craft wire; small American flag; two 1¼" wooden ball knobs; spray adhesive; and a hot glue gun.

Use hot glue for all gluing unless otherwise indicated.

1. Trace nose pattern, page 133, onto tracing paper; cut out. Use pattern to cut nose from one end of craft stick.
2. Paint nose and ball knobs flesh, stars yellow, and wooden hearts black; allow to dry.
3. Use compass to draw a 3¼" dia. circle on poster board; cut out. Glue circle to bottom of tube.
4. Apply spray adhesive to wrong sides of pants, shirt, face, and hat fabric pieces. Matching one edge of pants fabric to bottom edge of tube and overlapping ends at back, smooth around tube.
5. Overlapping edge of pants ½" and matching overlapped ends at back, smooth shirt fabric around tube. Repeat to apply face fabric, then hat fabric to tube.
6. For shoes, match points and glue small heart on top of large heart. Glue shoes to bottom of tube. Glue one ¾" dia. black button to each rounded edge of small heart.

7. Matching one long edge of hair to bottom edge of hat, glue hair to back of head. Glue eyes, nose, eyebrow, and beard to face. Use red marker to draw spirals on face for cheeks.
8. Fill plastic bag with sand; seal securely. Place bag in bottom of tube for weight.
9. Cut an 8" x 10" piece of poster board. Apply spray adhesive to wrong side of each 8" x 10" star-print fabric piece. Apply one fabric piece to each side of poster board.
10. Use compass to draw one 7" dia. circle and two 1¼" dia. circles on fabric-covered poster board; cut out. For hat brim, draw a 3¼" dia. circle in center of large circle. Using craft knife, carefully cut out inner circle for top of hat.
11. Slide hat brim over top of tube to seam between face and hat. Glue 3¼" dia. fabric-covered circle to top of hat. Overlapping ends at back, glue ribbon around hat.
12. For each arm, apply spray adhesive to wrong side of one 4½" x 6¾" fabric piece. Smooth fabric around tube. Using nail, punch two holes opposite each other ½" from one end (top) of tube.
13. Using nail, punch a hole on each side of body ½" below head.
14. To attach arms, bend ½" at one end of 7½" craft wire length to a 90° angle. Thread straight end of wire through holes in one arm, body, then remaining arm. Bend straight end of wire to a 90° angle to secure.
15. Glue one 1¼" fabric-covered circle over top end of each arm. Glue buttons to front of shirt and cuffs of sleeves.
16. For hands, glue flag stick across flat side of one ball knob. Glue 4"w star to center of 12" wire length; coil wire ends as desired. Glue one end of wire in hole of remaining ball knob. Glue knobs in ends of arms.
17. Adjust arms as desired and glue to body to secure.
18. Glue remaining stars to hat and wire at shoulder.

PATRIOTIC TABLE SET

Let's hear it for the red, white, and blue! Create a handy basket and silverware holder for your Fourth of July table by covering a shoe box and coffee can with commemorative fabrics. In no time, you'll have a "bang-up" way to arrange outdoor dining needs for a stars-and-stripes celebration.

PATRIOTIC PICNIC BOX

Recycled items: large shoe box, can for utensil caddy, and a white wire hanger.

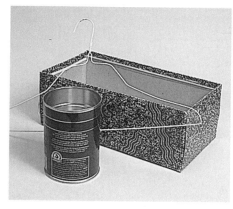

You will also need: desired fabrics, desired colors of ribbon in assorted widths, poster board, hammer, nail, wire cutters, pliers, spray adhesive, and a hot glue gun.

1. Follow *Covering a Box*, page 156, to cover outside of box.
2. To cover inside of box, measure inside height of box. Measure around inside of box; add ¹/₂". Cut a piece of fabric the determined measurement. Apply spray adhesive to wrong side of fabric piece. Beginning ¹/₂" past one corner, smooth fabric around inside of box.

3. Draw around bottom of box on wrong side of fabric; cut out along drawn line. Apply spray adhesive to wrong side of fabric. Glue fabric inside bottom of box.
4. Measure around box; add ¹/₂". Cut a length of ribbon the determined measurement. Overlapping ends at back, glue ribbon around box.
5. Tie several lengths of ribbon into a bow. Glue to front of box over ribbon.
6. To cover utensil caddy, measure around can. Measure height of can. Cut a piece of poster board to fit around can. Draw around poster board piece on wrong side of desired fabric. Cut out fabric ¹/₂" outside drawn lines. Apply spray adhesive to wrong side of fabric. Center poster board piece on

fabric piece. On one long edge, fold corners of fabric diagonally over corners of poster board. Leaving opposite long edge of fabric unturned, fold remaining edges of fabric over edges of poster board. With raw edge of fabric extending past top of can, hot glue wrong side of covered poster board around can. Glue excess fabric inside utensil caddy.
7. For handle, use hammer and nail to punch a small hole in each side of can near top edge. Cut hanger to desired length for handle. Thread one end of wire through each hole. Bend ends of wire to secure.
8. Measure around caddy; add ¹/₂". Cut a piece of ribbon determined measurement. Overlapping end at back seam, glue ribbon around caddy.

FESTIVE FALL VEST

*I*t's easy to transform
*an old menswear vest into a
festive and fun addition to your
fall wardrobe. With seasonal
appliqués finished in simple
embroidery stitches, this autumn
wearable will last all the way
through the months of changing
leaves, jack-o'-lanterns, and
bountiful harvests.*

HARVEST VEST

Recycled item: man's vest and assorted
buttons.

You will also need: paper-backed fusible
web, desired colors of felt, and desired
colors of embroidery floss.

1. Using patterns, page 137, follow *Making Appliqués,* page 157, to make five stem; three small pumpkin; two each of large pumpkin and star; and one each of moon, hat, face, shirt, pants, nose, and blackbird appliqués from felt.
2. Arrange appliqués on vest, overlapping as necessary; fuse in place.
3. Using desired color floss, work *Blanket Stitch,* page 159, around pumpkins, stars, hat, and edges of vest. Use desired color floss to work *Running Stitch,* page 159, along edges of moon, shirt, and pants; down center of face; and for mouth. Work a *French Knot,* page 159, at each end of mouth. Work a *Cross Stitch,* page 159, for each eye. Work *Straight Stitch,* page 159, for straw hands, feet, and hair.
4. Knotting floss at front, sew one button to each star.

WACKY HALLOWEEN WREATH

HALLOWEEN WREATH

Wish trick-or-treaters a "batty" Halloween with our frightful wreath! Constructed of spray-painted bubble wrap and fabric scraps, our wacky door decoration is a real treat. Accent this spooky project with foam packing peanuts and smashed can bats for a bewitching greeting.

Recycled items: 12-ounce aluminum beverage cans, wire clothes hanger, plastic bubble wrap, foam packing peanuts, and assorted fabric scraps.

You will also need: black spray paint, desired colors of spray paint (we used purple, orange, and bright green), black chenille stems, tracing paper, black plastic trash bag, desired colors of curling ribbon, white paper, two 6mm wiggle eyes and a smooth 6mm acrylic jewel for each bat, and a hot glue gun.

Allow paint to dry after each application.

1. Cut seventy-five 6" squares from bubble wrap and fabric scraps. Tear a 2¹/₂" x 28" strip of fabric for bow.

2. To bend a can for each bat, remove pop-top from can. Use both hands to hold can with thumbs below top rim and opening. Using thumbs, press on can to bend top rim down (Fig. 1). Turn can upside down and repeat to bend bottom of can in opposite direction. Step on can to flatten further.

Fig. 1

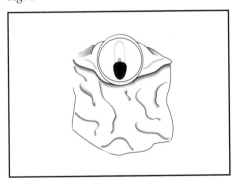

3. Shape wire hanger into a circle. Untwist wire at base of hook.

4. Spray paint hanger and cans black. Spray paint packing peanuts and several bubble wrap squares with desired colors.

5. Fold one bubble wrap square into quarters. Thread folded bubble wrap onto hanger by inserting one end of wire through bubble wrap near folded point. Repeat to cover entire hanger. Retwist wire at base of hook to secure bubble wrap.

6. Tie fabric strip into a bow around base of hook. Tie several lengths of curling ribbon into a bow around center of fabric bow.

7. For wings on each bat, cut a 8" x 10" piece from plastic trash bag. Match long edges to fold wing piece in half. Cut scallops along long, matched edges and short edges for tips on wings. Twist a chenille stem around center of folded wing piece; glue to back of can.

8. Cut two ¹/₂" triangles from plastic bag for ears; glue to top of can. Cut two fangs from white paper. Glue fangs inside edge of can opening. Glue jewel for nose and eyes to can.

9. Fold fabric squares into fourths. Glue fabric, bats, and painted packing peanuts to wreath as desired.

JACK-O'-LANTERN BUCKET

*Y*our favorite ghoul or goblin will love filling this jack-o'-lantern pail with treats on All Hallow's Eve. A snap to make from a three-liter soda bottle, the container is festive — and earth-friendly, too!

HALLOWEEN TREAT BUCKET

Recycled item: three-liter plastic bottle.

You will also need: orange spray paint, black electrical tape, clothespins, pushpin, black heavy-duty thread, tracing paper, black craft foam, 20" of 1¹/₄"w wired ribbon, and thick craft glue.

1. Mark around bottle 8" from bottom. Cut away top along mark.
2. For handle, cut a ³/₄" x 13" strip from top section of bottle. Trim each end to a point.
3. Spray paint outside of bottle; allow to dry.
4. Wrap handle and cover top edge of container with electrical tape.
5. Glue one end of handle to each side of container near top edge; secure with clothespins and allow to dry. Use pushpin to punch four holes through each end of handle into bottle (Fig. 1). Reinforce each end of handle by stitching an "x" through holes in handle and bottle.

Fig. 1

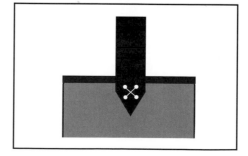

6. Trace patterns, page 130, onto tracing paper. Draw around patterns on craft foam; cut out shapes. Glue shapes to bottle. Tie ribbon into a bow; glue to one side of handle.

HOBGOBLIN TREAT BOXES

*A*ll the hobgoblins who visit your house will howl with delight when they receive Halloween handouts wrapped up in these spooky boxes! Created from clear plastic food containers, the packages are especially haunting when decorated with spiders and bats made from spools, beads, and bottle cups.

HALLOWEEN TREAT BOXES

Recycled items: clear plastic food containers with extended corner tabs, thread spool and large wooden bead for bat, and plastic bottle lid and button for spider.

You will also need: desired color spray paint for box, black spray paint, hole punch, assorted curling ribbon, and thick craft glue.
For Bat Treat Box, you will also need: tracing paper, black construction paper, two 5mm wiggle eyes, white acrylic paint, small paintbrush, and 1/4"w ribbon tied into a bow.
For Spider Treat Box, you will also need: two 5mm wiggle eyes, eight 2 1/2" pieces of

black chenille stem, and 1/4"w ribbon tied into a bow.

Allow paint and glue to dry after each application.

1. Paint outside of container with desired color spray paint. Using black spray paint, paint spool and bead for bat or bottle lid and button for spider. (*Note:* Follow Steps 2 and 3 for Bat or Steps 4 and 5 for Spider.)
2. Trace wing and ear patterns, page 133, onto tracing paper; cut out. Use patterns to cut two ears and one wing from construction paper. Refer to dashed line on pattern to fold tabs to back of ears.

3. Glue bead to spool, wings to back of spool, and ears and eyes to bead. Glue bow to bat. Center and glue bat on top of container. Use white paint to paint fangs.
4. For spider's legs, glue one end of each chenille stem inside edge of bottle lid. Bend chenille stems to form legs and feet.
5. Glue button and bow to bottle lid; glue eyes to button. Glue feet to top of container.
6. Punch one hole in each front corner tab of container. Fill container as desired. Tie several lengths of curling ribbon through holes to secure.

THANKSGIVING WREATH

Hang a ring of bountiful blessings in your home during the turkey-gobbling season! You can make our charming Thanksgiving creation from any wreath by attaching harvest motifs cut from fabrics that have been fused onto brown paper grocery bags. Finish the seasonal accessory with a natural raffia bow.

THANKSGIVING WREATH

Recycled items: brown paper bags and fabric scraps.

You will also need: paper-backed fusible web, black permanent fine-point marker, tracing paper, transfer paper, red colored pencil, curly twig wreath, raffia, and a hot glue gun.

1. Cut bags open along seams and press with a dry iron.
2. Using patterns, pages 138 and 139, follow *Making Appliqués,* page 157, to make three each of corn and corn husk appliqués; two each of eggplant, eggplant top, carrot, carrot top, pumpkin and pumpkin stem appliqués; and one each of hands, banner, dress, collar, hair, face, and bonnet appliqués from fabric.
3. Remove paper backing and arrange appliqués on bag, overlapping as indicated

on patterns; fuse in place. Leaving a ¼" border around each appliqué, cut out.
4. Trace "Give Thanks" design, page 138, onto tracing paper. Use transfer paper to transfer design to banner. Use marker to color design on banner; add details to face, bonnet, and hands; and draw "stitches" around each appliqué. Use colored pencil to draw cheeks on face.
5. Tie several lengths of raffia into a bow.
6. Arrange and glue appliqués and bow to wreath as desired.

"GIVE THANKS" SWAG

*S*hare thanks with family and friends when you hang our harvest swag in your home. You can salvage old paper bags to make padded fabric-covered cutouts. String them on a length of jute twine for a wholesome holiday festoon.

THANKSGIVING SWAG

Recycled items: brown paper bags, fabric scraps, and buttons.

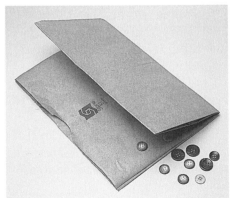

You will also need: paper-backed fusible web, tracing paper, transfer paper, red colored pencil, black permanent fine-point marker, polyester fiberfill, 72" of jute twine, compass, and a hot glue gun.

1. Cut bags open along seams and press with a dry iron.
2. Using patterns, pages 138 and 139, follow *Making Appliqués,* page 157, to make eggplant, eggplant top, carrot, carrot top, pumpkin, pumpkin stem, corn, corn husk, banner, hands, face, dress, collar, hair, and bonnet appliqués from fabric.
3. Remove paper backing and arrange appliqués on bag, overlapping as indicated on patterns; fuse in place. Leaving a 1/4" border around each appliqué, cut out.
4. Trace "Give Thanks" design, page 138, onto tracing paper. Use transfer paper to transfer design to banner. Use marker to color design on banner; add details to face, bonnet, and hands; and draw "stitches" around each appliqué. Use colored pencil to draw cheeks on face.

5. For backings, place each appliqué face down on plain side of remaining bag. Draw around each appliqué; cut out.
6. Center and glue Pilgrim backing on twine. Spacing 5" apart, glue remaining backings to twine.
7. For each appliqué, leave an opening for stuffing and use a fine line of glue to glue edges of appliqué over twine to backing. Stuff with fiberfill and glue opening closed.
8. For yo-yo patterns, use a compass to draw one 3" and one 5" circle on tracing paper; cut out. Using patterns and fabric scraps, follow *Making a Fabric Yo-Yo,* page 158, to make six of each size yo-yo.
9. Spacing as desired, glue gathered side of large yo-yos along twine. Glue flat side of one small yo-yo over twine to gathered center of each large yo-yo. Glue a button to center of each small yo-yo.
10. Glue a button to Pilgrim's collar.

"DE-LIGHT-FUL" DECORATIONS

*T*hese "de-light-ful" guys aren't just for lamps — this holiday season they'll also be busy brightening the tree! Our adorable Christmas ornaments are crafted from burned-out light bulbs topped with toddler-size socks for caps. Their whimsical faces are painted by hand.

LIGHT BULB ORNAMENTS

SNOWMAN

Recycled items: light bulb, white toddler-size sock, and a ³/₄" x 12" fabric strip.

You will also need: white spray paint, red and black acrylic paint, paintbrushes, desired color embroidery floss, ³/₄" dia. pom-pom, and a hot glue gun.

Allow paint to dry after each application.

1. Spray paint light bulb white.
2. Using red paint for nose and cheeks and black paint for eyes and mouth, paint face on bulb.
3. To make hat, roll cuff of sock to heel. Using six strands of embroidery floss, work *Running Stitch,* page 159, to secure cuff. Glue hat over base of light bulb and pom-pom to top of hat.
4. Tie fabric strip into a bow and glue to bottom of head.

ELF

Recycled items: light bulb and white toddler-size sock.
You will also need: flesh-color spray paint; tissue paper; red, green, and black acrylic paint; paintbrushes; flesh-color felt; desired color felt for bow tie; and a hot glue gun.

Allow paint to dry after each application.

1. Spray paint light bulb flesh.
2. Using red paint for cheeks and black paint for eyes and mouth, paint face on bulb.
3. To make hat, roll cuff of sock to heel. Lightly stuff hat with tissue paper and glue over base of light bulb. Alternating colors, paint red and green stripes around hat.
4. Trace bow tie, tie center, and ear patterns, page 135, onto tracing paper. Using patterns, cut two ears from flesh-color felt and bow tie pieces from desired color felt. Wrap tie center around bow; glue to secure. Glue tie to bottom of head and ears to sides of head.

OLD-TIMEY TIN PUNCH

Your Christmas tree will really shine when it's decorated with these folksy tin-punched ornaments! Mimicking a traditional craft, the designs are punched into juice can lids using a pushpin. Trimmed with fabric ruffles and twine, the lids are true country treasures.

TIN-PUNCHED ORNAMENTS

Recycled items: lids from large frozen juice cans, buttons, and newspaper to protect work surface.

For each ornament, you will also need: tracing paper, tape, pushpin, 2" x 26" strip of fabric for ruffle, 16" of jute twine, and craft glue.

1. For each ornament, trace desired pattern, page 135, onto tracing paper. Tape pattern to lid. Place lid on newspaper. Use pushpin to punch into lid through each dot on pattern. Remove pattern. .

2. For ruffle, matching wrong sides and long edges, press fabric strip in half. Stitching 1/4" from edge, baste along long raw edges of ruffle. Pull basting threads, gathering ruffle to fit lid. Glue gathered edge of ruffle to back of lid.

3. Beginning at top of lid, glue twine around edge of lid. Form a loop at top of lid for hanger. Glue button over ends of twine.

SODA BOTTLE SANTA WINDSOCK

*L*et the jolly old gentleman himself hang around your home for the holiday season with this homemade windsock. The top portion of a two-liter soda bottle forms Santa's head, and white trash bags are cut into strips to trim his hat and make his flowing "beard."

Recycled items: two-liter plastic bottle and a red button for nose.

You will also need: tracing paper, 7" x 20" piece of white fabric, 5" x 14" piece of red fabric, 4" square of muslin, black permanent medium-point marker, three 12" white chenille stems, white plastic trash bags, 1½ yds. of white cotton cord for hanger, craft glue, and polyurethane varnish.

1. Mark around bottle 2½" from bottom. Cut away bottom below mark.

2. For head, mark around bottle 6" from cut edge. Cut a 7" x 14" piece from white fabric. Apply glue to wrong side of fabric. Matching one long edge to mark on bottle, glue fabric around bottle. Smooth excess fabric over bottom edge and into bottle.

3. For hat, apply glue to wrong side of red fabric. Overlapping white fabric ¼", glue red fabric around bottle top. Gather fabric at bottle neck and fold excess fabric into bottle opening.

4. Trace face and mustache patterns, page 132, onto tracing paper. Use patterns to cut face from muslin and mustache from remaining white fabric. Apply glue to wrong sides of face and mustache. Overlapping as necessary, glue in place; allow to dry.

5. Use marker to draw eyes and eyebrows on face.

6. Allowing to dry after each application, apply three coats of varnish to fabric-covered areas.

7. Glue button to mustache.

8. For pom-pom on hat, cut twenty-eight 1½" x 4" rectangles from trash bag. Insert one end of one chenille stem through center of each rectangle (Fig. 1). Twist stem to gather rectangles at center of stem. Glue ends of stem into bottle.

Fig. 1

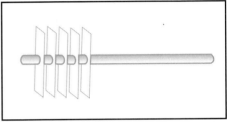

9. Cut sixteen 1½" x 20" strips from trash bags.

10. For hat trim, twist remaining chenille stems together end to end. Thread eight strips accordion-style onto chenille stems (Fig. 2). Wrap covered stems around bottom of hat; twist to secure. Adjust plastic strips to distribute folds evenly around hat and glue in place.

Fig. 2

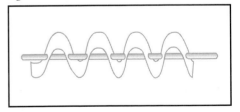

11. For streamers, glue one end of each remaining plastic strip inside bottom of bottle.

12. For hanger, tie cord around bottle neck; knot ends together at desired length.

BROWN BAG ANGEL

Angelic and easy to craft, this charming winged soul is the perfect accent for any holiday home. Created from "recycled" brown paper bags and crowned with natural raffia curls and a paper twist halo, the country-style angel will add a sweet touch to Christmas decorating.

PAPER BAG ANGEL

Recycled items: two large brown paper bags, one small brown paper bag, plastic sandwich bag with seal, sand, plastic grocery bags, rubber band, assorted fabric scraps, and assorted buttons.

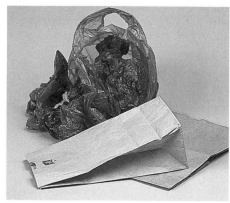

You will also need: paper-backed fusible web, white felt, embroidery floss, straight raffia, curly raffia, black permanent medium-point marker, 15" wired paper twist, tracing paper, and a hot glue gun.

1. For body, fill sandwich bag with sand; seal bag securely. Place sealed bag in one large paper bag for weight. Stuff plastic bags into paper bag to shape body. Gather top of paper bag closed. Secure with rubber band for neck.

2. Using pocket pattern, page 140, follow *Making Appliqués,* page 157, to make two pocket appliqués from fabric scraps. For apron, tear a 12" x 27" piece from fabric. With one long edge as top of apron, arrange and fuse pockets on apron. With seam of bag at back, gather top of apron around sides and front of neck. Secure gathers under rubber band.

3. For head, stuff small paper bag with plastic bags. Place opening of small bag over neck. Knot several lengths of straight raffia around neck to secure head. Tear a 1" x 11" fabric strip. Tie strip into a bow and glue to raffia knot.

4. Use marker to draw eyes and eyelashes.

For hair, glue lengths of curly raffia to head as desired. For halo, form paper twist into a 5" dia. circle; twist ends to secure. Glue ends to back of head.

5. Fold tracing paper in half. Matching tracing paper fold to blue line on pattern, trace wings pattern, page 140, onto tracing paper; cut out and unfold. Use pattern to cut one each from fabric, felt, and remaining paper bag. Place felt piece between wrong sides of fabric and paper bag pieces. Using embroidery floss, work *Running Stitch,* page 159, along edges to join layers. Use floss to make stitches through button holes. Glue wings to back of angel. Glue buttons to wings and body as desired.

CASUAL CHRISTMAS CANDLES

Candlelight adds toasty spirit to the most heartwarming season of all — Christmas! It's a snap to fill tin cans of different sizes with wax and decorate them with corrugated cardboard shapes, wooden buttons, and raffia. Our casual candles are at home anywhere during the holidays, whether displayed together or scattered around the room.

CHRISTMAS CAN CANDLES

Recycled items: various metal cans, corrugated cardboard, lightweight cardboard, and assorted wooden buttons.

You will also need: wood tone spray, pan to hold cans while melting wax, candle wax or paraffin, wax-coated wicks, tracing paper, transfer paper, twigs, raffia, and a hot glue gun.

1. Remove labels from cans.
2. Follow *Working with Wax,* page 158, to melt wax, fill cans to 1/4" below rim, and set wicks.
3. For each candle, measure around can. Determine desired height of covering for can. Cut a piece of corrugated cardboard the determined measurements; glue around can.
4. Spray lightweight cardboard and buttons with wood tone spray; allow to dry. Trace tree A and star patterns, page 146, onto tracing paper. Use transfer paper to transfer patterns onto lightweight cardboard. Cut out shapes and glue to cans as desired.
5. Center and glue twig to bottom of tree for trunk. Tie a length of raffia into a small bow; glue to top of tree.
6. Tie or glue raffia around cans as desired. Glue buttons to cans.

TIMEWORN STOCKINGS

You can enjoy the charm of an old-fashioned Christmas when you hang our home-style stockings. The vintage look is achieved by coffee-dyeing old unmatched socks. Once embellished with primitive designs, the stockings will become real mantel mementos!

SNOWMAN STOCKING

Recycled items: sock, fabric scraps, disposable aluminum pie pan, assorted buttons, and twigs.

You will also need: instant coffee, tracing paper, ecru and black felt, ecru and black embroidery floss, polyester fiberfill, 18" of black craft wire, pencil, and a hot glue gun.

1. Follow *Coffee Dyeing,* page 156, to dye sock.
2. Trace snowman and star patterns, page 131, onto tracing paper; cut out. Use pattern to cut snowman from ecru felt.
3. (*Note:* Use three strands of floss for all stitching.) Using black floss, work a *Cross Stitch,* page 159, for each eye and work *Satin Stitch,* page 159, for pipe. Using ecru floss and leaving an opening for stuffing, work *Blanket Stitch,* page 159, to sew edges of snowman to sock. Lightly stuff snowman with fiberfill and continue *Blanket Stitch* to close opening.
4. For hat, cut a 1¹⁄₂" x 2¹⁄₂" piece from black felt. For pom-pom, make several ¹⁄₂" long clips across one short edge of felt piece. Knot floss tightly at base of clips. Glue hat to snowman.
5. Cut two 2" twigs for arms. Insert one end of each twig between snowman and sock; glue in place. Cut a ¹⁄₂" twig for nose; glue in place.
6. For scarf, tear a ³⁄₄" x 12" strip of fabric. Tack one short end of strip to sock at each side of snowman's neck. Cut fabric strip in half; fray ends. Knot scarf at neck.
7. Use star pattern to cut six stars from pie pan. Use pencil to make indentations on stars as indicated by dots on pattern. Sew a button to center of each star.
8. For hanger, form a loop at center of wire; twist to secure. Coil each end of wire around pencil; remove from pencil. Tack base of loop to top edge of sock. Glue one star to each end of wire and one to base of loop. Glue remaining stars to stocking.
9. Sew buttons to snowman and stocking.

TREE STOCKING

Recycled items: sock, fabric scraps, assorted buttons, and dried orange peel.
You will also need: instant coffee, tracing paper, brown embroidery floss, pinking shears, jute twine, and a hot glue gun.

1. Follow *Coffee Dyeing,* page 156, to dye sock.
2. Use three strands of embroidery floss to work *Cross Stitch,* page 159, around heel and toe of sock.
3. For tree, tear the following strips from fabric: one ³⁄₄" x 5¹⁄₂", two ³⁄₄" x 2¹⁄₂", one ³⁄₄" x 2", and one ³⁄₄" x 1¹⁄₂".
4. Sew ³⁄₄" x 5¹⁄₂" strip to sock for tree trunk. Arrange and sew remaining strips to sock.
5. Stitching through button, fabric strip, and one layer of sock, sew desired buttons to tree.
6. For hanging loop, cut three 10" lengths of twine. Fold twine lengths in half, forming a 2¹⁄₂" loop. Tack base of loop to top edge of sock.
7. For orange peel hearts, trace pattern, page 131, onto tracing paper; cut out. Use pattern and pinking shears to cut five hearts from dried orange peel.
8. Cut five ¹⁄₂" squares of fabric; fray edges. Using six strands of floss and knotting floss on top of buttons, stitch through all layers to join a button and fabric square to center of each orange peel heart. Glue hearts to stocking as desired.

HOLLY STOCKING

Recycled items: sock, fabric scraps, and assorted buttons.
You will also need: instant coffee, two 5" x 8" pieces of paper-backed fusible web, two 5" x 8" pieces of fabric for leaves, one 5" x 8" piece of white felt, tracing paper, brown embroidery floss, jute twine, and a hot glue gun.

1. Follow *Coffee Dyeing,* page 156, to dye sock.
2. For cuff, measure around top of sock; add ¹⁄₂". Cut a strip of fabric 6"w by determined measurement. Matching long edges and wrong sides, press strip in half.
3. Use three strands of floss to work *Blanket Stitch,* page 159, along pressed edge. Overlapping ends at back of sock, fold raw edges of cuff into top of sock; sew in place. Use six strands of floss and *Straight Stitch,* page 159, to stitch desired message on cuff.
4. For leaves, fuse one web piece to wrong side of each piece of leaf fabric; remove paper backing. Fuse one leaf fabric piece to each side of felt piece. Trace leaf pattern, page 131, onto tracing paper. Use pattern to cut five leaves from fabric-covered felt. Use three strands of floss and *Running Stitch,* page 159, to stitch veins on leaves as desired.
5. For hanger, cut three 12" lengths of twine. Make a 2¹⁄₂" loop at center of one length of twine. Knot remaining lengths of twine around base of loop to secure. Tack knot to top edge of cuff.
6. Trim ends of twine to various lengths. Glue one holly leaf each to two twine ends. Thread desired buttons onto remaining twine ends; knot to secure. Glue remaining leaves to stocking. Sew buttons to stocking, leaves, and cuff as desired.

SANTA WREATH

Welcome holiday guests to your home with our sensational Santa wreath! Adorned with a string of old tree lights and cutouts from greeting cards, this dapper decoration is sure to spark Christmas cheer in folks who visit throughout the jingle bell season.

SANTA WREATH

Recycled items: artificial greenery wreath, a string of Christmas lights, and greeting cards.
You will also need: a hot glue gun.

1. (*Note:* Lights should not be illuminated.) Arrange and glue lights on wreath as desired. Secure cord to back of wreath.
2. Cut desired motifs from greeting cards. Arrange and glue motifs on wreath as desired.

FRAMED GREETING CARD

*T*ransform a tired flea-market bargain into an ornate gilded picture frame! By simply applying lace and glimmering gold paint to the wooden trim, you can easily create a rich Victorian-style border to surround a favorite holiday greeting card.

FRAMED GREETING CARD

Recycled items: frame, assorted flat lace trims, fabric scrap, cardboard, and a greeting card.

You will also need: gold spray paint, gold trim, 16" of wired gold ribbon, spray adhesive, and thick craft glue.

Use craft glue for all steps unless otherwise indicated. Allow paint and glue to dry after each application.

1. Cutting to fit at corners; glue trims to frame as desired.
2. Spray paint frame.
3. Measure width and height of opening on back of frame. Cut one piece each of cardboard and fabric the size of opening.

Use spray adhesive to glue wrong side of fabric to cardboard.
4. Using spray adhesive, center and glue greeting card on fabric-covered cardboard. Glue trim around edges of card as desired. Glue cardboard in frame.
5. Tie wired ribbon into a bow and glue to top center of frame.

make a spoonful of joy

Buttermilk Fudge
2 cups granulated sugar
1 cup buttermilk
½ cup butter or margarine
½ tablespoon corn syrup
1 teaspoon baking soda
1 teaspoon vanilla extract
½ cup chopped walnuts

candy * cake * fudge * cookies *

When you dress up your home for the holidays, don't forget the kitchen! A breeze to make, these inventive accessories are as useful as they are festive. Orphaned silverware pieces provide the body of a cute hanging angel, a unique recipe holder, and the handle for a nifty painted recipe box.

SPOON ANGEL

Recycled items: spoon and a small button.
You will also need: black permanent marker, 8" of 2¹/₂"w wired ribbon for dress, 8" of ¹/₂"w gold ribbon tied into a bow, tracing paper, 4" x 6" piece of muslin, 4" x 6" piece of batting, embroidery floss, curly raffia, 4¹/₂" of gold cord, 10" of clear thread, and a hot glue gun.

1. Use marker to draw eyes on back of spoon.
2. For dress, gather one long edge of wired ribbon around neck of spoon, overlapping ribbon ends at back of angel; glue to secure.
3. Glue bow to top center of dress. Glue button below bow.
4. Trace wings pattern, page 143, onto tracing paper. Use pattern to cut one each from muslin and batting. Use embroidery floss and *Running Stitch,* page 159, to sew muslin wings onto batting wings along rounded edge. Glue wings to back of angel.
5. For hair, glue several pieces of raffia around face.
6. For halo, loop cord and glue ends to back of head.
7. For hanger, knot ends of clear thread together and glue to back of head.

RECIPE CARD HOLDER

Recycled items: two salad forks.
You will also need: small wooden plaque for base; red, green, and gold acrylic paint; paintbrushes; fine sandpaper; silver paint pen; black permanent fine-point marker; and household cement.

Allow paint and household cement to dry after each application.

1. For base, paint plaque as desired.
2. For aged look, lightly sand edges of base. Use paint pen to accent edges of base.
3. Use marker to write desired message on base.
4. Bend each fork handle to a 90° angle. Center and glue handles to base.

RECIPE CARD FILE

Recycled items: recipe card file box and a spoon.
You will also need: tracing paper; transfer paper; red, green, and gold acrylic paint; paintbrushes; silver and gold paint pens; black permanent fine-point marker; wooden stars in assorted sizes; and household cement.

Allow paint and household cement to dry after each application.

1. Paint box as desired. Use gold acrylic paint to paint wooden stars.
2. Glue spoon to lid and stars in spoon.
3. Trace leaf, swirl, and star patterns, page 143, onto tracing paper. Use transfer paper to transfer patterns to box as desired. Use green paint to paint leaves. Use paint pens to paint swirls and stars.
4. Use paint pens to write desired message on box lid. Use marker to outline leaves and stars.

CHRISTMAS CARD SHUTTER

The louvers of a discarded wooden shutter are just right for showcasing holiday greeting cards! Apply bright paints and cute holiday appliqués to give country charm to this Yuletide project.

SHUTTER CARD HOLDER

Recycled items: wooden shutter (we used a 16" x 22" shutter), paper bags, old toothbrush, assorted fabric scraps, and assorted buttons.

You will also need: white, dark red, and blue acrylic paint; removable tape; paper towels; paper-backed fusible web; tracing paper; white felt; red and black permanent fine-point markers; red colored pencil; jute twine; and a hot glue gun.

Allow paint to dry after each application.

1. (*Note:* Slats must open to top of card holder.) Paint slats red and frame blue.
2. Cut a piece from paper bag to cover slats; tape in place.
3. To make snowdrift stencil, cut a piece from paper bag the same size as card holder. Draw a curved line for snowdrift several inches from one short edge of paper; cut along line. Tape snowdrift stencil to front of card holder, exposing bottom portion of frame.
4. Dip bristle tips of toothbrush into white paint, blot on paper towel to remove excess. Pull thumb across bristles to spatter paint on exposed portion of card holder. Repeat to achieve desired effect. Remove stencil.

5. Lightly spatter paint all blue areas.
6. Use patterns, page 136, and follow *Making Appliqués*, page 157, to make snowman; scarf; Santa's coat, hat, and mittens; and desired number of tree and star appliqués from fabric scraps. Make Santa's hat trim, pom-pom, beard, and coat trim appliqués from felt.
7. Overlapping as indicated on patterns, arrange and fuse appliqués on felt. Leaving a 1/8" felt border around Santa and snowman, cut shapes from felt.
8. Use black marker to outline snowman; draw arms, nose, and eyes on snowman; and draw arms and eyes on Santa. Use red marker to draw nose on Santa. Use red pencil to color cheeks on Santa and snowman.

9. Follow *Making a Bow,* page 158, to make a twine bow for top of card holder; glue in place. Glue a large star to center of bow.
10. Glue trees, Santa, snowman, and stars to cardholder as desired. Glue buttons to card holder as desired.
11. For banner, make a 1" x 1/2" appliqué of light-color fabric. Use black marker to write message on banner. Leaving a 3/4" border at top of banner appliqué, fuse appliqué to a 2" square of print fabric. Cut a length of twine 12" longer than distance between Santa's mitten and snowman's hand. Tie a bow at each end of twine. Centering banner between bows, fold and glue 1/2" of print fabric over twine. Glue bows to hands of Santa and snowman.

SOCK SNOWMAN

*H*e *may be a snowman,
but you'll never find a more
warmhearted fellow! Born of
a detergent bottle and a tube
sock, this cozy figure is outfitted
for winter fun. What better way
to make use of those odd socks!
Make one for yourself, but be sure
to fashion some extras to share.*

SOCK SNOWMAN

Recycled items: small dishwashing liquid
bottle with lid, terry-lined adult-size tube
sock, powder blush, sand, assorted fabric
scraps, and buttons.

You will also need: instant coffee,
2" dia. plastic foam ball, polyester fiberfill,
white sewing thread, black embroidery
floss, six 9" lengths of white cloth-covered
wire, pencil, tracing paper, black felt, and a
hot glue gun.

1. Fill bottle with sand; replace lid.
2. For head, make a hole in ball to fit lid.
Glue ball over lid.
3. Cut ribbing from sock. Follow *Coffee
Dyeing,* page 156, to dye ribbing.

4. For snowman, turn foot section of sock
inside out. Place bottle in sock. Stuff fiberfill
around bottle to shape snowman. Sew
opening closed at top of ball.
5. For cuff of hat, fold cut edge of ribbing
up 1" to right side; repeat. Tie a narrow
strip of fabric into a bow around top of
ribbing. Glue cuff of hat to head. Glue small
fabric scraps to hat as desired. Knotting
floss at front of buttons, sew buttons to hat
as desired.
6. For face, apply blush for cheeks. Cut
three small felt triangles for eyes and nose.
For each eye, use white thread to make a
single stitch in bottom corner of one
triangle. Glue eyes and nose to face. Use

embroidery floss and *Couching Stitch,*
page 159, to stitch mouth.
7. Trace mitten pattern, page 130, onto
tracing paper. Use pattern to cut four
mittens from felt.
8. For each arm, wrap three lengths of wire
around pencil. Remove from pencil and
shape as desired. Glue two mittens together
over one end of each arm. Sew one arm to
each side of snowman.
9. For scarf, cut a 1½" x 15" piece of
fabric. Tie scarf around neck. Clip ends of
scarf for fringe.
10. Knotting floss at front of buttons, sew
buttons to front of snowman.
11. Glue buttons to bottom of snowman
for feet.

Great GIFTS

The most heartwarming gifts are those that are handmade with love, no matter how simple they may be. Using items rescued from the waste can or recycling bin, you can whip up creative projects for lots of treasured people. Re-cover an old photograph album for a picture-taker on your list, or turn scraps of lace into frilly bookmarks for a favorite bookworm. For a good neighbor, present a handcrafted gift bag filled with scented country candles made from broken crayons and tapers. Friends and family will love your special offerings, and Mother Nature will appreciate your resourcefulness!

SPICED-UP CANDLES

*F*or our rustic candles, tapers that have seen better days are dipped in wax and then rolled in a mixture of spices. When gathered with a torn fabric bow, these candles make an appealing offering for a friend who enjoys country crafts.

SPICED CANDLES

Recycled items: taper candles, fabric strip, and newspaper to protect work surface.
You will also need: candle wax or paraffin, can 2" taller than candles for melting wax, pan to hold can while melting wax, ground spices, and aluminum foil.

1. Follow *Working with Wax,* page 158, to melt candle wax or paraffin.
2. Sprinkle a generous amount of spices on a sheet of aluminum foil.
3. For each candle, dip candle in melted wax, then roll in spices. Repeat until desired look is achieved.
4. Dip candle in wax to seal; allow to harden.
5. Tie fabric strip into a bow around candles.

WOODSY PAPER BAG ALBUM

*Y*ou can make a photograph album with woodsy appeal by simply covering an old album with brown paper grocery bags! The book is accented with a corrugated cardboard background displaying a silhouetted scene trimmed with twigs and wooden buttons for an outdoor touch.

PAPER BAG ALBUM

Recycled items: photo album with binding hardware on spine, two large paper bags, corrugated cardboard, lightweight cardboard, assorted wooden buttons, and twigs.

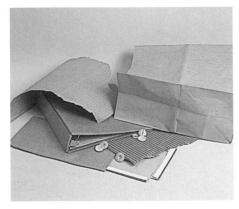

You will also need: tracing paper, wood tone spray, spray adhesive, and a hot glue gun.

Use hot glue for all gluing unless otherwise indicated.

1. Cut bags open at seams and press with a dry iron.
2. Draw around open album once on each bag. Cut out one bag 2" outside drawn lines. Apply spray adhesive to wrong side of bag.

Center open album on wrong side of bag piece. Fold corners of bag diagonally over corners of album; glue in place. Fold edges of bag over edges of album, trimming bag to fit 1/4" under binding hardware; glue in place.
3. Cut out remaining bag 1" inside drawn lines. Matching short edges, cut piece in half.
4. Apply spray adhesive to one side of each paper piece. With one edge under binding hardware, center and glue one paper piece inside front cover of album. Repeat to glue remaining piece inside back cover.

5. To decorate album cover, cut a piece from corrugated cardboard 1" smaller on all sides than front cover. Center and glue cardboard piece on front of album. Cut four twigs to fit around edges of cardboard; glue in place.
6. Trace patterns, page 146, onto tracing paper; cut out. Use patterns to cut one of each tree from lightweight cardboard and one moon and one star from corrugated cardboard. Spray cutouts with wood tone spray; allow to dry.
7. Arrange and glue cutouts and buttons on front of album. Cut pieces of twigs for tree trunks. Glue trunks under trees.

These linen accessories are perfect offerings for the woman who has everything! Covered with an antique dresser scarf, the padded hanger provides a delicate touch for an ordinary closet. The potpourri shoe sachets are made from vintage hankies and mismatched spoons. Inserting a small wind-up music box into a pillow that's easily made from another scarf adds a lovely tune to this ensemble of feminine fancies.

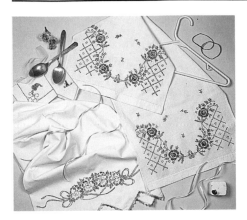

SHOE SACHETS

Recycled items: two handkerchiefs, two silver spoons, assorted ribbons, and silk flowers.
You will also need: batting, potpourri, and a hot glue gun.

1. For each sachet, cut a 6" circle of batting. Lay a handkerchief, wrong side up, on work surface. Center batting circle on handkerchief. Center bowl of spoon and a small amount of potpourri on batting circle.

2. Gather handkerchief at base of spoon handle. To secure handkerchief, tie several lengths of ribbon into a bow around gathers at base of handle. Glue silk flower to knot of bow.

MUSICAL PILLOW

Recycled items: dresser scarf with decorative edging and a wind-up music box.
You will also need: removable fabric marking pen, seam ripper, and polyester fiberfill.

1. Measuring from one narrow end, cut a 22" long piece from dresser scarf.

2. Determine exact center of scarf piece by folding into quarters. Make a small mark at folded point. At mark, work a buttonhole just large enough to insert handle of music box. Use seam ripper to open buttonhole.

3. Matching wrong sides and side edges of scarf piece, fold raw edge 1" past buttonhole. Fold decorative narrow edge to overlap raw edge 1/2"; pin in place. Sew side seams closed.

4. Place music box inside pillow and insert handle through buttonhole. Stuff pillow with fiberfill.

5. Use *Running Stitch*, page 159, to sew overlapped edges in place.

DECORATIVE HANGER

Recycled items: dresser scarf with decorative edging and a standard plastic clothes hanger.
You will also need: paper-backed fusible web, pressing cloth, and batting.

1. Trace around outside of hanger below hook twice onto paper side of fusible web. Draw a cutting line 1/2" outside slanted portions of hanger outlines and 1 1/2" below bottom lines; cut out.

2. For each side of hanger, position web piece on wrong side of scarf with straight edge of web 1/4" from decorative edge; fuse in place. Cut out scarf along edges of web piece; remove paper backing.

3. With pressing cloth on right side of stitched piece, fuse each stitched piece to batting. Trim batting to edges of stitched pieces.

4. Matching all edges, place right sides of stitched pieces together. Leaving bottom edges open and a 1/2" opening to insert hook of hanger at top, use a 1/4" seam allowance to sew pieces together along sides and top. Turn right side out. Insert hanger into opening.

FEATHERED FOAM TRINKETS

Transform plastic foam food trays into useful keepsakes that anyone will appreciate. A gilded heart becomes a standing frame for displaying a beloved photo, and small cutouts are used as coordinating accents on the Shaker box. The classic lines of the feather motifs are added by applying gentle pressure as you trace the patterns onto the foam. These trinkets will make great gifts any time of the year.

FOAM TRAY ACCESSORIES

Recycled items: foam food trays and a decorative button for box.

You will also need: tracing paper, stylus or dull pencil, metallic gold paint, small paintbrush, and craft glue.

For frame, you will also need: photograph, poster board, 15" of gold and white cord, and 3½" of desired ribbon.

For box, you will also need: Shaker box (we used a 2¾"h x 6" dia. box with lid), gold cord, and desired ribbon.

FRAME
1. Trace frame pattern, page 141, onto tracing paper.
2. Place pattern on foam tray. Use stylus or pencil to trace all lines of pattern onto foam tray. Cut out frame along outside and center opening lines.
3. Allowing foam to show through, lightly paint right side of foam piece; allow to dry.
4. Glue photograph to poster board.
5. Centering opening over photograph, trace around frame on poster board. Cut out ⅛" inside lines; glue to back of frame.
6. Glue cord around opening.
7. For frame stand, cut a 1" x 5" piece of poster board. Score and bend poster board 1" from one end. Center and glue bent end of stand ¾" below top edge of frame back.

To stabilize stand, center and glue ¾" of one end of ribbon to center of wrong side of stand. Center and glue ¾" of opposite end of ribbon to back of frame.

BOX
1. Trace feather and medallion patterns, page 141, onto tracing paper.
2. Place pattern on foam tray. Use stylus or pencil to trace all lines of pattern onto foam tray. Cut out shapes along outside lines. Glue poster board to frame.
3. Allowing foam to show through, lightly paint right side of foam shapes; allow to dry.
4. Center and glue medallion to lid. Arrange and glue feathers around lid. Glue button to medallion and cord around medallion. Glue cord and ribbon to box as desired.

SPLENDID SUN CATCHERS

*B*ring colorful rays of sunshine into a friend's home with our easy-to-make sun catchers! Reminiscent of stained glass, these window ornaments are crafted from clear plastic food containers backed with tissue paper. The designs from nature are outlined with black dimensional paint and colored with thinned acrylic paints.

SUN CATCHER GIFTS

Recycled items: clear plastic food containers.

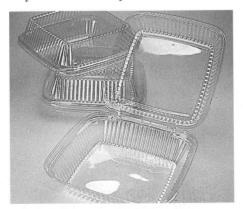

You will also need: black permanent medium-point marker, black dimensional paint, white tissue paper, desired colors of acrylic paint, paintbrushes, pushpin, clear thread, clear bugle beads, and craft glue.

1. For each sun catcher, cut a flat piece from plastic container. Use marker to trace desired pattern, pages 147 - 149, onto front of plastic piece.
2. Using equal parts water and glue, thin glue. Glue tissue paper to back of plastic piece; allow to dry.
3. Use dimensional paint to paint over lines on front of plastic piece; allow to dry.

4. Using equal parts water and acrylic paint, thin paint. Using dimensional paint lines as a guide, paint tissue paper; allow to dry.
5. Cut out along outer lines of design.
6. Use pushpin to make a small hole in top of sun catcher. Insert thread through hole and string beads to desired length for hanger; knot ends.

*B*oth decorative and useful, our homemade vinegars are a tasty offering. The zesty condiments are simple to prepare, and they're ideal for flavoring salads, sauces, and more. Old candles and crayons can be melted to make colorful seals for the lids, and your gift tags can be cut from previously used cards and stationery. Raffia ties and greenery make an impressive finish.

Recycled items: glass bottles with lids, candle pieces for wax seal on bottle, crayon pieces to color wax, can for melting wax, greeting card or stationery for tags, and newspaper to protect work surface.

You will also need: ingredients listed for desired herbal vinegar, funnel, pan to hold can while melting wax, raffia, items to decorate outside of bottles (we used eucalyptus, pepper grass, boxwood, and twigs), hole punch, black permanent fine-point marker, craft glue, and a hot glue gun.

1. Wash bottles and lids. Sterilize by boiling in water for five minutes; allow to dry.
2. Follow recipe to prepare and bottle vinegar.
3. For wax seal, follow *Working with Wax,* page 158, to melt candle and crayon pieces to 2" deep.
4. Allowing wax to harden slightly between coats, dip top of bottle in wax to completely coat lid.
5. For each tag, cut a 2" square from desired card or paper. Tear a slightly smaller square from coordinating paper.

Using craft glue, center and glue smaller square on 2" square. Punch hole near one corner of tag. Use marker to write message on tag.
6. For each bottle, knot several lengths of raffia around bottle neck. Hot glue decorative items to knot as desired. Thread one end of raffia through hole in tag and knot to secure.

HERBAL LEMON VINEGAR

    4 lemons
    4 small sprigs fresh dill, basil, *or* tarragon
    4 cups white wine vinegar

Peel each lemon in a continuous spiral. Place lemon peel and herbs in bottles. In a medium saucepan, heat vinegar to boiling. Pour into bottles. After sealing bottles, chill at least 2 days to allow flavors to blend. Store in refrigerator.
Yield: about 32 ounces vinegar

HERBAL WINE VINEGAR

    1   cup white vinegar
    1/2 cup dry red wine
    1   teaspoon dried rosemary leaves, crushed
    1/2 teaspoon garlic powder
        Fresh rosemary sprig

In a small bowl, combine vinegar, wine, dried rosemary, and garlic powder. Place rosemary sprig in bottle. Pour vinegar mixture into bottle. After sealing bottle, shake well. Refrigerate 8 hours to allow flavors to blend. Store in refrigerator.
Yield: about 12 ounces vinegar

"UNCANNY" GIFT CANS

*H*ere's an "uncanny" way to surprise a great gardener! Not your ordinary garden tools, these cute containers are constructed using food cans and cardboard — and they're just the right size for delivering jars of homemade preserves or pickles. Decorated with seed packet motifs, our cheery "can-tainers" make truly pleasing presents.

DECORATIVE WATERING CANS

Recycled items: cans, lightweight cardboard, wire hanger for handle (optional), large button for end of spout (optional), and a seed packet for label.

You will also need: tracing paper, grey spray primer, silver spray paint, several 12" lengths of raffia, craft glue, and a hot glue gun.

For can with wire handle, you will also need: hammer, small nail, wire cutters, and pliers.

Allow primer, paint, and glue to dry after each application. Use hot glue for all gluing unless otherwise indicated.

1. If wire handle is desired, use hammer and nail to punch a small hole in each side of can near top edge. Cut hanger to desired length for handle. Thread one end of wire through each hole. Bend ends of wire to secure.

2. Trace desired handle and spout patterns, page 142, onto tracing paper; cut out. Use patterns to cut handle and spout from cardboard.

3. Glue cardboard handle and spout to can and button to spout.

4. Spray watering can with primer, then with paint.

5. Cut front from seed packet. Use craft glue to glue packet front to front of can.

6. Tie raffia into a bow; glue to can.

48

FLANNEL SHIRT BLANKET

*F*lannel shirts are cuddly to wear, and they make an even cozier blanket! Our throw is a cinch to make from squares of flannel cut from worn shirts and sewn to thermal fleece. Great for warming up cold fingers and toes, this clever quilt offers a warm surprise for a chilly pal.

FLANNEL SHIRT THROW

Recycled items: flannel shirts (we used six large shirts) and 56 buttons.

You will also need: 63" x 69" piece of thermal fleece, embroidery floss, pearl cotton (optional), and needle.

1. Wash and dry all fabrics before beginning project.
2. Baste edges of fleece 1/2" to wrong side. Using pearl cotton or six strands of embroidery floss, work *Blanket Stitch,* page 159, to secure basted edges.
3. For flannel top, cut forty-two 9" squares from shirts. Using a 1/4" seam allowance, sew seven squares into a row; repeat to make six rows. Matching right sides and seams, sew rows together along long edges.
4. Baste edges of flannel top 1/4" to wrong side. Center top on fleece. Using three strands of embroidery floss and *Running Stitch,* page 159, sew edges of flannel top to fleece.
5. Using three strands of floss and knotting floss on top of buttons, stitch through all layers to sew one button at each seam intersection.

FLORAL DECOUPAGED BASKET

Here's a simple gift idea for a friend who needs a pretty place to keep odds and ends. Splashed with colorful fabric cutouts and topped with a padded lid, an old basket becomes a convenient storage container. The loop-and-button closure provides easy access for stashing or retrieving items.

Recycled items: wicker basket, heavy cardboard, buttons, and beads.

You will also need: pickling gel (we used cactus green), paintbrush, fabric with floral motifs, matte decoupage sealer, foam brush, ruler, pencil, heavy-duty thread, polyester fiberfill, 1/4"w ribbon, and a hot glue gun.

Allow pickling gel and decoupage sealer to dry after each application.

1. Follow manufacturer's instructions to paint basket with pickling gel.

2. Cut desired floral motifs from fabric. Use sealer and follow *Decoupage,* page 157, to apply motifs to basket. Apply a thin coat of sealer over entire basket.

3. To make lid, draw around basket opening on cardboard; cut out. Using pencil, make a hole at center of cardboard.

4. To cut fabric cover for lid, place cardboard on wrong side of fabric. Determine distance from edge of cardboard to center hole; add 1". Use new measurement to draw a line on fabric parallel to corresponding edge of cardboard (Fig 1). Cut out fabric along drawn line.

Fig. 1

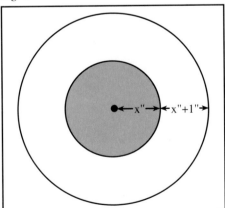

5. Using heavy-duty thread and *Running Stitch,* page 159, baste edge of fabric piece 1/4" to wrong side. Center cardboard on wrong side of fabric. Cover top of cardboard with fiberfill before pulling thread to gather fabric at center of lid.

6. Join a button on top of lid to a button on bottom of lid with several tight stitches through hole in center of lid (Fig. 2).

Fig. 2

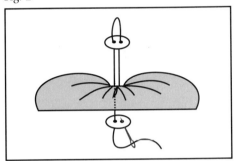

7. For hinge, cut a 3" square of fabric. Glue one edge of square to bottom of lid and opposite edge inside back of basket.

8. For closure, thread a needle with heavy-duty thread. Beginning inside front of basket at desired location for closure, thread needle through a button inside basket, basket, a bead, large flat button, small flat button, and a second bead. Stitch back through buttons, bead, basket, and inside button. Repeat to stitch several times; tie thread ends inside basket.

9. Measure distance from bottom button on lid to closure on basket. Double the measurement; add 2". Cut a length of ribbon the determined measurement. Knot ends of ribbon together to form a loop. Slide knotted ends of loop under button on bottom of lid and pull tightly to secure. Slip loop over closure.

BIRTHDAY SURPRISE CAN

You've heard of a message in a bottle, but what about a gift in a can? An embellished juice can is an unexpected way to present someone with a special surprise. Include a can opener as part of the topper so the lucky recipient can uncover the wonderful treat you pack inside!

GIFT IN A CAN

Recycled items: large can and heavy cardboard.

You will also need: desired gift (we recommend using a lightweight gift), card stock or heavy colored paper, photocopy of label design on page 145, markers, can opener, 23" of desired ribbon, stick glue, and a hot glue gun.

1. Use can opener to remove one end from can. Wash and dry can.
2. Measure around can; add ¹/₂". Measure height of can. Cut a piece from card stock the determined measurements. Overlapping ends at back, glue card stock around can.
3. Use markers to color photocopy of label; cut out. With opening at bottom, use stick glue to glue label on front of can.
4. Draw around bottom of can on cardboard; cut slightly inside drawn line. Place gift in can and hot glue circle in opening.
5. Tie ribbon into a bow around can opener handle. Hot glue bow to top of can.

CANDY FLOWERPOTS

These gifts certainly have sweet beginnings! The painted flowerpots were once pint-size ice-cream containers. Putting together the bright blooms is a breeze using stirring straws, fabric scraps, and buttons. Filled with candy, the pots make delightful surprises for special people.

CANDY FLOWERPOTS

Recycled items: pint-size ice-cream containers with lids, fabric scraps, buttons, and corrugated cardboard.

You will also need: spray primer, terra-cotta spray paint, tracing paper, compass, black acrylic paint, small paintbrushes, floral foam, construction paper for leaves and sign, stirring straws, black permanent fine-point marker, candy, and thick craft glue.
For bee design, you will also need: transfer paper and white and yellow acrylic paints.
For dotted design, you will also need: pencil with unused eraser and a cotton swab.

Allow primer, paint, and glue to dry after each application.

1. Spray container and lid with primer, then with terra-cotta paint.
2. For dotted container, use cotton swab, pencil eraser, and black paint to paint random dots. Paint zigzag design on edge of lid as desired.
3. For bee container, trace bee design, page 143, onto tracing paper. Use transfer paper to transfer design onto container. Use acrylic paints to paint design. Paint bee trails on container and stripes on edge of lid as desired.
4. For flower pattern, use compass to draw a 5" circle on tracing paper; cut out. Use flower pattern and follow *Making a Fabric Yo-Yo,* page 158, to make flower. With one end of straw at center of flower, glue straw between gathers for stem. Glue button to center of flower. Repeat to make desired number of flowers.
5. Trace leaf pattern, page 143, onto tracing paper; cut out. Use leaf pattern to cut desired number of leaves from green construction paper. Glue leaves to stems.
6. For sign, cut a 2" square from cardboard. Cut a 1 3/4" square from construction paper. Use marker to write desired message on construction paper square. Center and glue construction paper square on cardboard square. Insert one end of a straw between layers of cardboard; glue in place.
7. Cut a piece of floral foam slightly smaller than inside of container; glue in place.
8. Insert flowers and sign into floral foam. Covering foam, fill container with candy.

RESOURCEFUL COUNTRY CANDLES

54

For friends who love the charm of the country, tuck a handmade candle in an embellished gift bag. Just melt broken tapers or crayons with paraffin to make colored wax and pour it into glass jars; push wicks in before the wax hardens and then add your handwritten labels to the jars. Deliver the thoughtful offerings in gift bags decorated with buttons, fabric scraps, and raffia. How delightfully resourceful!

GIFT BAG AND COUNTRY CANDLES

GIFT BAG

Recycled items: brown paper gift bag (we used a 8" x 10½" bag), fabric scraps, and a button.

You will also need: photocopy of tag design on page 146, colored pencils, paper-backed fusible web, raffia, black permanent fine-point marker, and a hot glue gun.

1. Cut the following pieces of fusible web: one 2½" x 4", one 3" x 4½", one 5" x 7", and one 6" x 8". Cut out photocopy of tag.
2. Fuse 2½" x 4" web piece to wrong side of tag. Fuse remaining web pieces to wrong sides of desired fabrics. Trim fabrics to edges of web pieces; remove paper backings. Arranging from largest to smallest, center and fuse fabric pieces on one side of bag. Center tag on fabric pieces; fuse in place.
3. Use pencils to color tag as desired. Use marker to draw stitches on bag around fabric and write message on tag.

4. Use raffia and follow *Making a Bow,* page 158, to make desired size bow. Glue bow above tag. Use raffia to stitch through holes in button. Glue button to center of bow.

BASIC CANDLE

Recycled items: glass jar, canning lid and ring to fit jar (optional), crayons or broken candles, can for melting wax, and newspapers.

You will also need: candle wax or paraffin, desired candle scent, pan to hold can while melting wax, and wax-coated wick.

1. Follow *Melting Wax,* page 158, to prepare wax. Follow manufacturer's instructions to add candle scent.
2. Follow *Setting Wicks and Pouring Wax,* page 158, to fill jars and set wicks.

PAINTED STAR CANDLE

Recycled items: fabric and batting scraps.

You will also need: Basic Candle, tracing paper, enamel paint, compressed craft sponge, pinking shears, black permanent fine-point marker, and a hot glue gun.

1. Trace star pattern, page 145, onto tracing paper; cut out. Use pattern to cut star from sponge. Follow *Compressed Sponge Painting,* page 159, to paint jar; allow to dry. Using marker, outline stars and draw "stitches" as desired.
2. To cover lid, draw around jar lid on batting and wrong side of fabric. Cut out batting circle ½" outside drawn line. Use pinking shears to cut out fabric circle 3" outside drawn line.
3. Replace lid on jar. Center and glue batting on lid. Measure around neck of jar; add 8". Tear a strip of fabric ½"w by the determined measurement. Center fabric circle over lid. To secure fabric circle, tie fabric strip into a bow around neck of jar.

VANILLA CANDLE

Recycled items: fabric scraps, and assorted buttons.

You will also need: Basic Candle, page 55, tracing paper, paper-backed fusible web, desired color of acrylic paint, compressed craft sponge, photocopy of tag design, page 146, black permanent fine-point marker, colored pencils, white felt, embroidery floss, and a hot glue gun.

1. Measure around neck of jar; add 6". Tear a strip of fabric 3/4"w by the determined measurement. Knot strip around neck of jar.
2. Leaving a 1/4"w border, cut out tag. Use colored pencils to color tag. Use marker to write scent of candle on tag. Center and glue tag on front of jar.
3. Trace star pattern, page 145, onto tracing paper; cut out. Use pattern to cut star from sponge. Using acrylic paint, follow *Compressed Sponge Painting,* page 159, to paint one star on fabric; allow to dry. Apply fusible web to wrong side of fabric behind painted shape. Cut out star along painted lines. Fuse star to felt. Leaving a 1/8"w felt border, cut out star and glue to knot of fabric strip.
4. Stitch embroidery floss through holes in buttons; glue button to jar as desired.

FABRIC STAR AND HEART CANDLE

Recycled items: fabric scraps, poster board, and assorted buttons.

You will also need: Basic Candle, page 55; tracing paper, paper-backed fusible web, white felt, desired colors of acrylic paint, compressed craft sponge, raffia, pinking shears, black permanent fine-point marker, embroidery floss, craft glue, and a hot glue gun.

1. For fabric piece around jar, determine desired height for fabric. Measure around jar; add 1/2". Cut a piece of fabric the determined measurements. Overlapping ends at back, glue fabric around jar.
2. For jar lid, trace around metal insert on fabric and poster board; cut out. Using craft glue, glue fabric to poster board. Place metal insert, fabric-covered poster board, and ring on jar.
3. Trace star and heart patterns, page 145, onto tracing paper; cut out. Use patterns to cut star and heart from sponge. Using acrylic paint, follow *Compressed Sponge Painting,* page 159, to paint desired number of stars and hearts on fabric; allow to dry. Apply fusible web to wrong side of fabric behind painted shapes. Cut out shapes along painted lines. Fuse shapes to felt. Leaving a 1/8"w felt border, cut out shapes.
4. Use marker to draw "stitches" along edges of shapes. Alternating stars and hearts and spacing shapes evenly around jar, glue shapes to fabric strip.
5. Stitch embroidery floss through holes in buttons; glue one button to center of each star or heart.

PAINTED HEART CANDLE

Recycled items: one button.

You will also need: Basic Candle, page 55, photocopy of lid design on page 146, black permanent fine-point marker, colored pencils, tracing paper, two colors of enamel paint, compressed craft sponge, pencil with unused eraser, raffia, and a hot glue gun.

1. Use colored pencils to color lid design. Center opening of lid ring over lid design. Use a pencil to lightly draw around outside edge of ring; cut out along drawn line. Place metal insert, lid design, and ring on jar.
2. Trace heart pattern, page 145, onto tracing paper; cut out. Use pattern to cut heart from sponge. Follow *Compressed Sponge Painting,* page 159, to paint hearts on jar. Use pencil eraser to paint dots between hearts; allow to dry. Use marker to outline hearts and dots and draw patchwork "stitches" across outlines as desired.
3. Tie several lengths of raffia into a bow around neck of jar. Tie a length of raffia through holes in one button. Glue button over knot of bow.

COUNTRY BERRY CANDLE

Recycled items: fabric scraps and assorted buttons.

You will also need: Basic Candle, page 55, raffia, pinking shears, photocopy of tag design on page 146, black permanent fine-point marker, colored pencils, paper-backed fusible web, white felt, embroidery floss, and a hot glue gun.

1. For fabric piece around jar, determine desired height for fabric. Measure around jar; add 1/2". Cut a piece of fabric the determined measurements. Overlapping ends at back, glue fabric around jar.
2. To cover lid, draw around jar lid on wrong side of fabric. Use pinking shears to cut out circle 3" outside drawn line. Replace lid on jar. Center fabric circle over lid. To secure fabric circle, knot several lengths of raffia around neck of jar.
3. Leaving a 1/4"w border, cut out tag. Use colored pencils to color tag. Use marker to write scent of candle on tag. Center and glue tag on front of jar.
4. Using star pattern, page 145, follow *Making Appliqués,* page 157, to make one star appliqué from fabric. Fuse star to felt. Leaving a 1/8"w felt border, cut out star and glue to jar.
5. Stitch embroidery floss through holes in buttons; glue buttons to jar as desired.

STATIONERY KEEPER

A favorite pen pal will love this "notable" idea for storing stationery! The perfect gift for anyone who enjoys putting pen to paper, our box has lots of room for paper and envelopes. The desktop keeper is simple to construct from a detergent box, and it will be as useful as it is decorative.

STATIONERY KEEPER

Recycled items: small detergent box and a button.

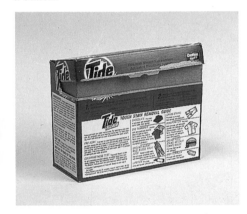

You will also need: fabric, ruler, craft knife, ribbon, spray adhesive, and a hot glue gun.

1. Refer to Fig. 1 to cut top from box.

Fig. 1

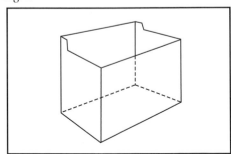

2. Follow *Covering a Box,* page 156, to cover box with fabric.

3. Measure around box. Cut a length of ribbon the determined measurement.

Beginning at front of box, hot glue ribbon around box. Hot glue button over ends of ribbon.

These handy totes are a nifty way for kids to carry along their toys! Milk jugs and vinegar bottles make sturdy bottoms, while drawstring tops provide lots of room and easy closing. Kids will love the fun styles of these totes, and parents will appreciate their usefulness.

Recycled items: one-gallon plastic containers and assorted buttons.

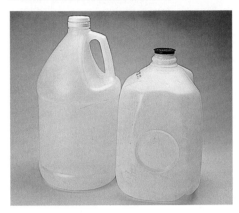

You will also need: craft knife, small hole punch, desired fabric for bucket top, two 1 yd. lengths of $1/4$"w ribbon, embroidery floss, and a small safety pin to thread ribbon through casing.

For personalized bucket, you will also need: paper-backed fusible web; fabric for letters, border, and label background; 2"h alphabet stencils; black permanent fine-point marker; and thick craft glue.

1. (*Note:* We cut our round container 6" from bottom and our square container $3^{3/4}$" from bottom.) Cut container to desired height. Spacing holes approximately $1/2$" apart, punch an even number of holes $1/4$" below cut edge of container.

2. For fabric top, measure around cut edge; add $1/2$". Cut a piece of fabric $11^{1/2}$" by the determined measurement. Matching right sides and using a $1/4$" seam allowance, sew $11^{1/2}$" ends together to form a tube.

3. With seams at center back and leaving 3" between top edge and buttonhole, work a $1/2$" buttonhole on each side of tube for drawstring holes.

4. For casing, press top edge of tube $1/4$" to wrong side. Turn pressed edge $1^{3/4}$" to wrong side again, to cover buttonholes;

press. Stitch around tube 1" below top edge and along inner pressed edge. Turn fabric tube right side out.

5. Press raw edge of fabric tube $1/2$" to wrong side.

6. To attach fabric to container, place bottom edge of fabric top over container to cover holes. Using floss and beginning inside container, stitch through one hole, fabric, a button, back through button, and through fabric into next hole. Repeat to attach buttons around container. (Fig. 1).

Fig. 1

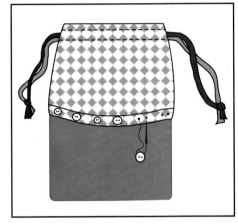

7. For drawstrings, use safety pin to thread a length of ribbon into one buttonhole, through casing, and out through same buttonhole. Repeat to thread remaining ribbon through opposite buttonhole. Knot ribbon ends together on each side of fabric.

8. To make label for personalized container, use stencils to trace desired letters in reverse on paper side of fusible web. Fuse traced letters to wrong side of letter fabric; cut out. Remove paper backing and arrange letters on right side of background fabric. Cut label to desired size. Center and glue label on front of container. Cut four $1/2$"w strips from border fabric to cover edges of label; glue in place.

9. Use marker to draw stitch marks around letters and along edges of label.

TUNES TOTE

*H*elp your favorite music lover take some tunes on the road with this clever carrying case! Simply decoupage a detergent box with magazine cutouts of recording stars for an upbeat look. A rope handle completes the project.

COMPACT DISC TOTE

Recycled items: detergent box with fold-down lid, index or business card, pictures cut from magazines, and four buttons.

You will also need: silver spray paint, spray varnish, two lengths of ribbon for trim on box and box lid, rope for handle, craft knife, black embroidery floss, black permanent fine-point marker, and craft glue.

Allow paint, varnish, and glue to dry after each application.

1. Remove handle from box.
2. Spray paint box and card silver.
3. Following *Decoupage*, page 157, glue desired magazine pictures onto box.
4. For trim on lid, glue ribbon along edges of lid. Glue ends to wrong side of lid.
5. For trim on box, glue ribbon along sides and front of top edge of box.
6. For handle, cut rope to desired length. Apply glue to ends to prevent fraying.
7. To attach each end of handle, use craft knife to cut a small hole in side of box at desired height for handle. Thread a needle with floss. Beginning inside box, thread needle through one button, hole in box, one end of rope, and second button. Thread needle back through second button, rope, box, and first button; repeat several times. Pull ends of floss tight and knot inside box.
8. For each mini compact disc on handle, cut a 1" dia. circle from painted card. Use marker to draw a dot at center and a circle around each dot. Glue a mini compact disc to each button on handle.

HEARTFELT STAMP

*W*rap forget-me-not remembrances in very personal style with hand-decorated gift paper and cards fashioned with your own exclusive designs. You can stamp unique motifs on plain wrapping paper, gift bags, and greeting cards. Pieces cut from plastic foam trays become reusable stamps in just a few easy steps.

HEART STAMP

Recycled items: two plastic foam trays and a gift bag or greeting card (optional).

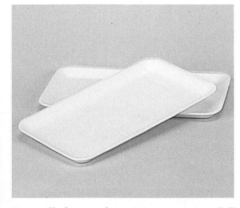

You will also need: tracing paper, tape, dull pencil, craft knife, red and pink acrylic paint, paintbrushes, desired paper for stamping, gold paint pen; 6¼" x 11" piece of colored paper, hole punch, and 18" of ¼" ribbon for card; 5" x 6" piece of colored paper and pinking shears for bag; and craft glue.

Allow paint and glue to dry after each application.

1. For stamp, trace stamp pattern, page 132, onto tracing paper. Tape pattern on one foam tray. Use pencil to trace over lines on pattern to transfer design to foam tray.
2. Use craft knife to cut out heart and border along transferred lines. Cut a 4½" x 5½" flat piece from remaining foam tray. Glue foam heart and border to flat foam piece.
3. Place paper to be stamped on a flat, smooth surface. Use paintbrushes to apply paint to heart and border. Press painted design onto paper. Repeat to stamp paper as desired.

4. Use paint pen to add lines and swirls to stamped designs as desired.
5. For card, fold colored paper in half lengthwise. Cut one design from stamped paper. Center and glue design on one side of colored paper. Punch two holes near folded edge of card. Thread ribbon through holes: tie into a bow.
6. For bag, cut out design from stamped paper. Center and glue design on colored paper. Trim edges of colored paper with pinking shears. Center and glue colored paper to bag.

With utensils in tow, this celestial kitchen helper is ready to watch over a special cook. No one would ever guess that underneath her angelic attire is a two-liter soft drink bottle!

KITCHEN ANGEL

Recycled items: two-liter soda bottle with lid, sand to weight bottle, white sock, and assorted buttons.

You will also need: instant coffee, 15" of ⁷⁄₈"w pre-gathered trim, 6" of ³⁄₈"w flat trim, ¹⁄₂ yd. of ¹⁄₄"w ribbon, 2¹⁄₄" x 3" plastic foam egg, black permanent fine-point marker, powder blush, curly doll hair, fabrics for dress and apron, tracing paper, polyester fiberfill, brown embroidery floss, 9" x 12" piece of ecru felt, small basket with handle (we used a 3"w by 5"h basket), items to fill basket (we used miniature kitchen items), and a hot glue gun.

Use ¹⁄₄" seam allowances for all sewing steps. Use two strands of floss for all running stitches.

1. Fill bottle with sand; replace lid.
2. Follow *Coffee Dyeing,* page 156, to dye sock and trim pieces.
3. For head, make a hole in large end of foam egg to fit lid. Place egg, large end first, in toe of sock. Gather sock at small end of egg; trim excess fabric. Overlap and glue cut edges to egg.
4. Use marker to draw eyes, nose, and mouth on head. Use blush to color cheeks.
5. For hands, cut a 1¹⁄₄" x 4" piece from excess sock fabric. Matching long edges and right sides, fold sock piece in half. Sew along each raw edge; cut in half widthwise. Turn each hand right side out.
6. From apron fabric, cut one 7" x 8" piece for apron skirt and one 2¹⁄₂" x 4" piece for apron bib.
7. Press one short edge and each long edge of apron skirt ¹⁄₄" to wrong side. Press one long edge and each short edge of apron bib ¹⁄₄" to wrong side. Work *Running Stitch,* page 159, to secure each pressed edge of apron bib and skirt.
8. Cut a length of gathered trim ¹⁄₂" longer than bottom edge of apron skirt. Press each end ¹⁄₄" to wrong side. Glue trim along wrong side of bottom edge of apron skirt.
9. From dress fabric, cut two 4" x 6" pieces for sleeves, two 4" x 8¹⁄₂" pieces for yoke, and one 9¹⁄₂" x 23" piece for skirt.
10. For each arm, match right sides and long edges of sleeve fabric piece; sew long edges together. Turn sleeve right side out. Fold one edge of sleeve ¹⁄₂" to wrong side. Insert hand into folded end of sleeve; glue in place. Knot a length of floss around wrist to gather sleeve. Lightly stuff arm with fiberfill. Glue a length of trim around wrist, covering floss.
11. For yoke front, matching long raw edges, center and baste apron bib to right

side of one yoke piece. Sew one button to each top corner of bib.
12. Make a small pleat in raw end of each arm, baste to secure.
13. Center and pin pleated edge of each arm to one short edge on right side of yoke front. Matching right sides and raw edges of yoke pieces, sew short edges together through all layers.
14. For skirt, matching raw edge of apron skirt to one long edge of dress skirt, center and baste apron skirt to right side of dress skirt. Matching right sides and short edges, sew skirt together. Press bottom edge of skirt ¹⁄₄" to wrong side. Work *Running Stitch* to secure pressed edge.
15. Sew two rows of gathering threads along top edge of skirt. Gather skirt to fit bottom edge of yoke. Matching right sides, raw edges, and apron skirt to apron bib, sew gathered edge of skirt to yoke.
16. Press remaining top edge of dress yoke ¹⁄₄" to wrong side. Baste along pressed edge. Place dress over bottle. Pull threads to gather dress around neck of bottle; knot thread to secure.
17. Overlapping ends at back of neck, glue a length of gathered trim around bottom edge of bottle cap.
18. Using wings pattern, page 142, follow *Making Patterns,* page 156, to trace wings onto tracing paper. Use pattern to cut two wings from felt. Matching edges of wings, work *Running Stitch* along edges to join layers. Sew a button at tip of each wing. Glue wings to back of dress.
19. Glue head to lid. Arrange hair as desired and glue in place. Tie ribbon into a bow around head; glue to secure.
20. Glue one hand to bottom edge of apron skirt. Place basket handle on opposite arm. Bend arm and glue to secure. Glue desired items into basket.

BEACHCOMBER FRAMES

*S*hip ahoy! Give your first mate a cool way to keep those summer beachcombing memories alive with our fun, clever frames. To make the neat gifts, we poured plaster into the bottoms of old milk jugs with cookie cutters or cans providing the opening shapes. We then embellished them with favorite ocean finds and sailing motifs. These seashore show-offs are just right for framing pictures of those sun-filled days of carefree water play!

FUN FRAMES

Recycled items: large plastic container with flat bottom, cookie cutter or can to shape photograph opening, poster board, and small seashells or rope.

You will also need: craft knife, craft wire to bind ends of rope, aluminum foil, plaster of paris, desired colors of acrylic paint, paintbrush, black permanent fine-point marker, desired photograph, decorative plate stand (optional), and thick craft glue.

1. For mold, cut around container 2" from bottom edge. Cover cookie cutter or can with foil; center in bottom of container.
2. If rope border is desired, cut rope to fit along inside edge of mold with ends meeting. Wrap wire around ends of rope to prevent fraying. Place rope in mold.
3. Follow manufacturer's instructions to prepare plaster. Pour plaster ¾" deep around cookie cutter or can. If desired, arrange shells in plaster.
4. Allow plaster to set 24 hours.
5. Remove plaster by carefully flexing mold. Remove can or cookie cutter from plaster.
6. Paint frame as desired; allow to dry. Use marker to add details.
7. Glue photograph to poster board. Centering photo in frame opening, draw around frame. Cut out ½" inside drawn line and glue to back of frame.
8. If desired, place on stand.

EXQUISITE BIBS

Gifts for baby are even more special when they're handmade from the heart. These delicate bibs are created from scraps of vintage fabric with decorative edging. In just a few easy steps, you'll have exquisite baby bibs — and the best part is that they were created with love!

BABY BIBS

Recycled item: vintage fabric with decorative edging.

For each bib, you will also need: tracing paper, fabric for backing (optional), 24" of ½"w double fold bias tape, and 7" of ¼"w ribbon (optional).

1. Fold tracing paper in half. Aligning folded edge of paper with blue line of pattern, trace pattern for desired size bib, page 150, onto tracing paper. Cut out pattern through both layers of paper; unfold. Align bottom edges of bib pattern with decorative edges of fabric (Fig. 1); cut out bib front. (*Note:* For bib with decorative edge backing, follow Step 2. For bib with contrasting backing, follow Step 3.)

Fig. 1

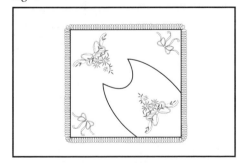

2. Place bottom edges of bib pattern ¼" inside decorative edges of remaining fabric; cut out.

3. Use bib pattern to cut piece from backing fabric. Press bottom edges of bib backing

⅛" to wrong side; repeat. Stitch along pressed edges to secure.

4. Matching raw edges and right sides, use a ¼" seam allowance along side edges to sew bib front to bib backing. Turn right side out and press.

5. To bind neck opening, center and enclose raw edge of bib in bias tape with narrow side of tape on right side of bib. Beginning at one end on right side of bib and stitching through all layers, sew edges of bias tape together.

6. If desired, tie ribbon into a bow and tack to bib.

CRAFTY CADDIES

*P*resent a super stitcher or tidy tool man with the gift of organization! A four-pack beverage carrier is ideal for carting jars and cans filled with project necessities. Personalize the caddies with glued-on fabric or the pocket from an old pair of jeans.

SEWING AND TOOL CADDIES

Allow paint and glue to dry after each application. Use hot glue for all gluing steps unless otherwise indicated.

SEWING CADDY
Recycled items: beverage carrier (we used a four-pack size), heavy cardboard, jars with lids and cans to fit into carrier, small container with lid to use as pin box, and buttons.
You will also need: yellow spray paint, wood tone spray, desired fabrics, tracing paper, white and yellow felt, black permanent fine-point marker, pinking shears, half of a 2" dia. plastic foam ball, spray adhesive, and a hot glue gun.

1. For added support, cut a piece of cardboard the size of carrier bottom. Glue cardboard to bottom of carrier.

2. Spray paint pin box, jar lids, and inside of carrier yellow; allow to dry. Lightly spray painted surfaces with wood tone spray.

3. Measure around carrier. Measure height of carrier sides. Add 2" to each measurement. Cut a piece of fabric the determined measurements. Spray wrong side of fabric piece with spray adhesive. With fabric extending 1" beyond top and bottom edges, glue fabric around carrier. Clipping as necessary, smooth excess fabric over edges.

4. For handle cover, fold a sheet of tracing paper in half. With fold of paper at top edge of handle, trace shape of handle onto tracing paper. Cut out and unfold pattern (Fig. 1). Use pattern to cut handle cover from felt. Use spray adhesive to glue felt to handle.

Fig. 1

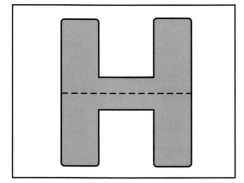

5. For each can, measure height of can. Measure around can; add 1/2". Cut a piece of fabric determined measurement. Use spray adhesive to glue fabric around can.

6. Trace bee wings, sunflower, sunflower center, and sunflower leaf patterns, page 140, onto tracing paper. Use tracing paper patterns to cut two centers and two leaves from desired fabrics. Cut three sunflowers and three bee wings from felt. Glue one each of sunflower, center, leaf, and bee wings to front of carrier. Repeat on

back of carrier.

7. For pin box, trace around top of box on wrong side of desired fabric. Use pinking shears to cut out fabric piece 1/4" inside line. Use spray adhesive to glue fabric piece to top. Glue bee wings to fabric.

8. For each bee, glue a button to bee wings for body. Use marker to draw bee trail, antennas, and desired lines on wings.

9. For pincushion jar, wrap a 5" square of fabric around foam piece; glue fabric edges to flat side of foam. Glue remaining sunflower to jar lid. Center and glue covered foam on sunflower.

TOOL CADDY

Recycled items: beverage carrier (we used a four-pack size), heavy cardboard, denim

jeans, jars with lids, and cans to fit into carrier.

You will also need: blue spray paint, grey fleck stone spray paint, tracing paper, blue felt, desired fabric, spray adhesive, and a hot glue gun.

1. Using blue paint to paint inside carrier and grey paint to paint remaining items, follow Steps 1 - 5 of Sewing Caddy to cover caddy, jars, and cans.

2. Remove a small pocket and a belt loop from jeans. Leaving top edge open, glue edges of pocket to front of carrier. Leaving enough space under loop to insert desired tool, glue ends of belt loop to one side of carrier.

FLORAL BOUQUET ALBUM

Offer a shutterbug a pretty way to organize pictures of cherished people and events by reviving an old photograph album with a new fabric cover. A cheerful spray of spring flowers gathered with a scrap of shiny satin ribbon makes this appealing album a treasure that any picture-taking fan will want to share!

FLOWER BOUQUET ALBUM

Recycled items: photo album with binding hardware on spine, poster board, and silk flowers.

You will also need: batting, fabric, 20" of 1"w wired ribbon, spray adhesive, and a hot glue gun.

Use hot glue for all gluing unless otherwise indicated.

1. Draw around open album on batting and wrong side of fabric. Cut out batting along drawn line. Cut out fabric 2" outside drawn lines.

2. Use spray adhesive to glue batting to outside of closed album. Center open album on wrong side of fabric piece. Fold corners of fabric diagonally over corners of album; glue in place. Fold edges of fabric over edges of album, trimming fabric to fit ¹/₄" under binding hardware; glue in place.

3. Draw around front of album twice on poster board and wrong side of fabric. Cut out poster board pieces ¹/₂" inside drawn lines. Cut out fabric pieces 1" outside drawn lines.

4. Apply spray adhesive to wrong side of one fabric piece. Center one poster board piece on fabric piece. On one long edge, fold corners of fabric diagonally over corners of poster board. Leaving opposite long edge of fabric unturned, fold edges of fabric over edges of poster board. With raw edge of fabric under binding hardware, center and glue wrong side of covered poster board inside front of album. Repeat for inside back cover.

5. Arrange and glue flowers to front of album. Tie ribbon into a bow and glue in place.

FRILLY BOOKMARKS

A devoted reader will never lose her place when you present her with these beautifully embellished bookmarks. Accented with ribbon, paper doilies, and golden trinkets, the frilly page keepers will be reminders of your thoughtfulness every time she opens her books.

DECORATIVE BOOKMARKS

Recycled items: colored paper, motifs cut from wrapping paper, paper ribbon, pieces of paper doily, ribbon, and charms.

You will also need: clear self-adhesive plastic, small hole punch, and craft glue.

1. Arrange and glue paper ribbon, doily pieces, and motifs on colored paper in desired shape for bookmark; cut out bookmark.

2. Cut two pieces of plastic 1/2" larger than bookmark. Remove paper-backing from one plastic piece. Center and smooth bookmark onto plastic. Remove backing from second piece. Matching edges, smooth second piece of plastic over remaining side of bookmark. Press plastic together around edges of bookmark and trim 1/8" from edge of bookmark.

3. For each bow on bookmark, punch two holes near edge of bookmark. Thread a length of ribbon through holes to front of bookmark. If desired, thread a charm onto ribbon. Tie ribbon into a bow.

4. Glue additional ribbon and charms to bookmark as desired.

Home Sweet SPRUCE-UPS

*Y*our house will feel even more
like a home when it's accented with
decorative accessories that show off
your own distinctive touch! With very
little expense, you can totally redo
— or simply renew — your decor
with our easy but fabulous ideas. It's
a cinch to decoupage an ordinary
footstool with vintage handkerchiefs
or a picture frame with pretty paper
napkins. Create pillows with pizzazz
from worn denim jeans or old table
scarves. You can even dress up a
nondescript chair with colorful
paints and contemporary fabric to
make a real conversation piece. The
possibilities for inventive home
decor are endless!

CREATIVELY PAINTED CHAIR

*A*n orphaned chair becomes a conversation piece when it's painted with diverse patterns and colors and finished with a new fabric seat cover. This project has infinite design possibilities, so you can't go wrong! Just choose some favorite paint hues and fabric and let your creativity flow.

PAINTED LADDERBACK CHAIR

Recycled item: wooden chair.

You will also need: items listed under *Preparing an Item for Painting or Decoupage* on page 157, spray primer, desired colors of acrylic paint, assorted paintbrushes, spray varnish, kraft paper, fabric to cover seat, batting, and a staple gun.

Allow primer, paint, and varnish to dry after each application.

1. If necessary, remove seat from chair.
2. Follow *Preparing an Item for Painting or Decoupage* to prepare chair.

3. Apply primer to chair. Paint desired colors on chair (we painted sections of the legs and uprights alternating colors).
4. Use pencil to draw designs on chair (we drew triangles, zebra stripes, leopard spots, starbursts, and wavy lines). Paint designs as desired.
5. Apply two or three coats of varnish to chair.
6. For seat cover, draw around seat on kraft paper. Cut out kraft paper 3" outside drawn line for pattern. Use pattern to cut several pieces from batting. Cut a piece of fabric 3" outside pattern edge.
7. Layer batting pieces, then fabric piece on seat. Fold fabric corners diagonally over batting to fit seat corners. Alternating sides, pulling taut, and trimming excess as necessary, staple edges of fabric to bottom of seat. Reattach seat to chair.

COFFEE CAN TABLE

*D*on't trash your three-pound coffee cans, because we've found a great way to transform them into a new table! By stacking the plaster-weighted cans and then covering them with wallpaper, you construct four "legs" that will support a purchased glass top. The last step is deciding what to display on your new piece of furniture!

COFFEE CAN TABLE

Recycled items: sixteen large coffee cans with lids (we recommend using cans from one brand for uniform size).

You will also need: plaster of paris, duct tape, one-sided corrugated cardboard, wallpaper and wallpaper border, tracing paper, felt, desired top for table (we used a 16" x 60" piece of shatterproof glass with finished edges), household cement, and spray adhesive.

Use household cement for all gluing unless otherwise indicated. Allow cement to harden after each application.

1. For each can, follow plaster manufacturer's instructions to fill can with plaster to a depth of 1"; allow to harden. Glue lid on can.

2. For each leg, stack and glue four cans together. Wrap duct tape around each seam to secure. Measure height of leg. Measure around leg. Cut a piece of cardboard the determined measurements. Apply spray adhesive to corrugated side of cardboard. Wrap cardboard around leg. Use duct tape to cover seam.

3. Measure height of leg. Measure around leg. Cut a piece of wallpaper the determined measurements. Measure around leg. Cut a piece of wallpaper border the determined measurement.

4. Apply spray adhesive to wrong side of wallpaper and border pieces. Wrap wallpaper around leg. Beginning at wallpaper seam and matching one long edge with top edge of leg, glue border around leg.

5. Draw around end of one leg on tracing paper; cut out. Use tracing paper pattern to cut eight circles from felt. Use spray adhesive to glue a felt circle to each end of each leg.

6. Positioning one leg under each corner of tabletop, place tabletop on legs.

Vintage linens can be found in lots of charming prints, and our felt pillows are an easy way for you to salvage the undamaged portions of old tablecloths, napkins, and other pieces. Whether you discover them in the attic or at the flea market, these heirloom cloths offer their own special air of nostalgia. Simple embroidery stitches bring the antique linen and soft new felt of our pillows together for a feminine finish.

SQUARE PILLOW

Recycled items: vintage fabric (we used a tablecloth) and assorted buttons.
You will also need: tracing paper, two 14" felt squares, one 10" felt square, embroidery floss, and polyester fiberfill.

1. Trace large and small scallop patterns, page 144, onto tracing paper; cut out. Fold one 14" felt square in half from top to bottom and again from left to right. Matching straight edges of large scallop pattern to folded edges of felt, cut along scalloped edges of pattern through all layers. Repeat for remaining 14" square.
2. Fold 10" felt square in half from top to bottom and again from left to right. Matching straight edges of small scallop pattern to folded edges of felt, cut along scalloped edges of pattern through all layers.
3. Cut one 7¼" square from fabric. Press each edge ¼" to wrong side.
4. Center and baste fabric square on small felt square. Center corners of small felt square on edges of one large felt square and baste in place. To join layers, use three strands of floss to work *Blanket Stitch,* page 159, along edges of fabric square. Remove basting threads. Sew one button at each corner of small felt square.
5. Matching edges and wrong sides, baste large felt squares together. Using three strands of floss and leaving an opening for stuffing, work *Running Stitch,* page 159, 2" inside edges to join felt squares.
6. Stuff pillow with fiberfill. Continue *Running Stitch* to stitch opening closed.

ENVELOPE PILLOW

Recycled items: vintage fabric (we used a tablecloth) and assorted buttons.
You will also need: tracing paper, two 11" x 13" felt pieces, one 8" x 13" felt piece, embroidery floss, 24" of flat trim, and polyester fiberfill.

1. Trace scalloped flap and fabric flap patterns, page 144, onto tracing paper; cut out.
2. Matching short edges of 8" x 13" felt piece, fold in half. Matching dashed line of scalloped flap pattern to folded edge, cut along scalloped edge of pattern through all layers. Use three strands of floss to work *Running Stitch,* page 159, ⅛" from scalloped edge.
3. Cut an 8" x 12" fabric piece. Matching short edges, fold in half. Matching dashed line of fabric flap pattern to folded edge of fabric, cut fabric along curved line of pattern through all layers.
4. Matching straight edges, center and baste fabric flap on scalloped flap. Stitching through all layers, sew trim over curved edge of fabric flap.
5. Matching straight edges, place flap between large felt pieces. Being careful to catch only the long edge of flap in seam allowance and leaving an opening for turning, use a ½" seam allowance to sew felt pieces together.
6. Turn right side out and stuff with fiberfill. Sew opening closed. Sew buttons to flap as desired.

PARTY NAPKIN PICTURE FRAME

*S*ave those paper party napkins left over from a special get-together and use them to dress up a battered picture frame. Party supplies come in a variety of artistic designs that are just perfect for decorating projects. We chose floral napkins for our decoupaged frame. The painted and colorwashed frame is given an antique finish for a classic look.

NAPKIN DECOUPAGED FRAME

Recycled item: picture frame.

You will also need: white spray paint, color wash spray (we used peach), brown antiquing gel, paper napkins with floral motifs, foam brush, gold rub-on metallic finish, spray varnish, and craft glue.

Allow paint, gel, varnish, and glue to dry after each application.

1. Spray paint frame white. Lightly spot-spray frame with color wash.

2. Follow manufacturer's instructions to apply antiquing gel to frame.
3. Cut floral motifs from napkins.
4. Mix one part water to one part craft glue; apply glue to frame. Arrange motifs on frame as desired; smooth in place.
5. Follow manufacturer's instructions to highlight frame with metallic finish.
6. Spray frame with varnish.

COVERED OTTOMAN

An elegant yet simple project, this fabric-covered ottoman is a classy way to make something new out of something old. Drape your choice of decorative material over a layer of batting and staple everything to an old ottoman or footstool. Attaching deep fringe trim to the bottom edge makes a spectacular finish.

COVERED OTTOMAN

Recycled item: ottoman or footstool.

You will also need: batting, fabric, heavy-duty staple gun, fringe, screw-on wooden feet or legs (optional), and a hot glue gun.

1. If ottoman has feet or legs, remove before beginning.

2. Refer to Fig. 1 to measure from bottom edge on one side of ottoman to opposite bottom edge; add 6".

Fig. 1

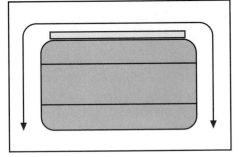

3. To cover a square ottoman, use measurement determined in Step 2 to cut three squares of batting and one square of fabric. To cover a round ottoman, follow *Cutting a Fabric Circle*, page 157, and use one-half the measurement determined in Step 2 as the string measurement to cut three batting circles and one fabric circle.

4. Center one piece of batting over top of ottoman. Pulling batting taut over ottoman and gathering excess at corners, use staple gun to staple edges of batting to underside of ottoman. Repeat for remaining batting pieces and fabric cover.

5. Attach feet near bottom corners of ottoman.

6. Measure around ottoman; add 1". Cut a length of fringe determined measurement. With fringe just touching floor, glue base of fringe around ottoman.

"TEE-RIFIC" GOLF BALL LAMP

A "tee-rific" addition to an office or bedroom, our golf lamp will score a hole in one! A large canning jar filled with balls and tees becomes the base for a purchased lamp kit. Covering a plain lampshade with tailored plaid and trimming it with gold cording creates a unique table accent that any duffer will love!

GOLF BALL LAMP

Recycled items: one-gallon glass jar with lid, golf balls to fill jar and for feet, golf tees, and a lampshade.

You will also need: 6" dia. wooden plaque for base, desired color acrylic paint for base, paintbrush, lamp kit for bottle base, tissue paper, ruler, removable tape, desired paper or fabric to cover lampshade, gold cord, household cement, spray adhesive, and a hot glue gun.

Allow paint and household cement to dry after each application. Use household cement for all gluing unless otherwise indicated.

1. Paint plaque for base.
2. Spacing evenly along bottom edge, glue three golf balls to bottom of base for feet. Glue bottom of jar to top of base. Fill jar with golf balls and tees.

3. Follow manufacturer's instructions to attach lamp kit to lid. Replace lid on jar.
4. Follow *Covering a Lampshade,* page 158, to cover shade.
5. Beginning at back of lamp, hot glue gold cord around bottom edge of jar. Tie a second piece of gold cord around top of shade as desired; knot and trim ends.

GOLFER'S COFFEE TABLE

*O*ur sporty trunk is perfect "fore" use as a coffee table or at the foot of a golfer's bed. Not only is it an inventive decorative accent, but it's also great for hiding things away. The project is child's play to do — just cover an old trunk with prepasted wallpaper and decoupage it with pictures cut from magazines.

GOLF TRUNK

Recycled item: trunk.

You will also need: items listed under *Preparing an Item for Painting or Decoupage* on page 157, prepasted wallpaper, two colors of acrylic paint to coordinate with wallpaper, small paintbrushes, photocopies from desired magazines, wood tone spray, rub-on metallic finish, four wooden bun feet, drill to attach bun feet, spray varnish, and spray adhesive.

Allow paint, wood tone spray, and varnish to dry after each application.

1. Follow *Preparing an Item for Painting or Decoupage* to prepare trunk. Use one color paint to paint sides of trunk. Use remaining color paint to paint bun feet and trim on trunk.
2. To attach each foot, position foot under corner of trunk as desired. Using drill bit slightly smaller than screw for foot, drill a hole through trunk into center of foot. Drive screw through hole into foot.
3. Cut 1/2" strips of wallpaper for bottom edges of lid and bottom edges of trunk. Trimming to fit around hardware, follow manufacturer's instructions to apply wallpaper to top of trunk and strips to edges.
4. Follow manufacturer's instructions to apply metallic finish to hardware.
5. Spray photocopies with wood tone spray. Cut out photocopies and apply spray adhesive to wrong sides. Arranging as desired, apply photocopies to trunk.
6. Apply two or three coats of spray varnish to trunk.

*H*ere's a way to "recycle" those brown paper grocery bags! Easily assembled using poster board, fabric pieces, and paper towel tubes, the fun project replicates an old-fashioned patchwork design. In no time, you'll have a charming wall hanging that will add a homespun touch to any nook or cranny.

Recycled items: two large brown paper bags, 12" square of poster board, four paper towel tubes, and four buttons.

You will also need: paper-backed fusible web, fabrics (we used four prints), black permanent fine-point marker, 6" of craft wire, and a hot glue gun.

1. Cut grocery bags open along seams, press with a dry iron.
2. For background, fuse a 12" square of web to one bag. Trim bag to edge of web. Remove paper-backing and fuse to poster board.
3. (*Note:* Small quilt blocks are cut from large quilt block.) Using patterns, page 149, follow *Making Appliqués,* page 157, to make eight leaf, four flower, and one 4¼" square appliqués from desired fabrics. Make one 6" square appliqué; do not remove paper backing.
4. For large quilt block, arrange 4¼" square, flower, and leaf appliqués on 6" square, overlapping as necessary; fuse in place.

5. Cut quilt block into four 3" squares, remove paper backing. With a ¼" space between squares, arrange and fuse squares on center of background. Use marker to draw "stitches" around squares. Glue buttons to flower centers.
6. For frame, slightly flatten paper towel tubes. Cut one 7" section and one 2½" section from each tube. Cut four 6" x 9" pieces of fabric to cover 7" sections. Cut four 5" x 6" pieces of fabric to cover 2½" sections.
7. For each tube section, overlap ends at back and glue fabric around tube. Folding excess fabric to a point at each end; glue ends to back of tube. Glue tube sections to background.
8. For bow, cut one 3" x 18" strip, one 2½" x 5" strip, and two 3" x 20" strips from remaining bag.
9. For loops, overlap short edges of long strip ½" and glue in place. Fold each long edge of short strip ½" to one side. With seam of loops at center back and overlapping short ends of short strip at back, wrap short strip around long strip to gather center of bow; glue to secure.
10. For each streamer, cut a "V" in one end of a remaining strip. Make a pleat at center of straight ends; glue to back of bow.
11. Glue streamers to back of frame. For hanger, loop craft wire through back of bow; twist ends to secure.

COWBOY LAMP

Rustle up an old pair of blue jeans and use them to create our Western lamp! A purchased lamp kit makes it easy to transform a two-liter plastic soda bottle into a fun way to light up a room. After the bottle is covered with a cut-off jeans leg, a pocket and bandanna are glued on. A lampshade decorated with pictures of the Old West rounds up this project with cowboy style!

WESTERN LAMP

Recycled Items: two-liter plastic bottle, sand to weight bottle, denim jeans, lampshade, and pictures from magazines.

You will also need: lamp kit for bottle base, 1 yd of ¹/₂" dia. rope, bandanna, heavy white paper, braided jute trim, spray adhesive, and a hot glue gun.

Use hot glue for all gluing unless otherwise indicated.

1. Fill bottle with sand. Follow manufacturer's instructions to attach lamp kit to bottle.

2. Remove one back pocket from jeans and cut a 16" section from bottom of one leg.
3. To cover bottle, place leg piece over bottle with hem at bottom edge of bottle. Fold top edge 2" to wrong side. Wrap rope around jeans leg 1" below top edge to gather jeans around bottle neck; glue ends of rope in place.
4. Glue side and bottom edges of pocket to front of lamp. Arrange and glue bandanna in pocket.

5. Use spray adhesive to glue pictures to heavy paper. Trim edges of paper even with pictures. Use spray adhesive to glue pictures to shade as desired.
6. Measure around top edge of shade; add ¹/₂". Cut a length of trim the determined measurement. Overlapping ends at back, glue trim along top edge of shade. Repeat to add trim to bottom edge of shade.

POSY POCKET PILLOW

S et the mood for smiles and comfort with this appliquéd denim pillow. Using fabric scraps and worn-out blue jeans, you can create a padded "pocket full of posies" for any casual room.

BLUE JEAN PILLOW

Recycled items: denim jeans and four ¹/₂" dia. buttons.

You will also need: two 16" squares of fabric for pillow front and pillow back, paper-backed fusible web, tracing paper, fabrics for appliqués, white embroidery floss, and polyester fiberfill.

1. Wash and dry all fabrics.
2. Use patterns, page 143, and follow *Making Appliqués,* page 157, to make four flower and seven leaf appliqués.
3. Remove one back pocket from jeans. Center pocket near bottom edge on right side of pillow front; pin in place. Arrange appliqués, overlapping as necessary, on pillow front. Remove pocket and fuse appliqués in place.
4. Follow *Machine Appliqué,* page 158, to sew along edges of appliqués.
5. Trace flower center pattern, page 143, onto tracing paper. Use pattern to cut four flower centers from jeans.
6. Reposition pocket on pillow front. Leaving top edge open, sew side and bottom edges of pocket to pillow front. Knotting floss at front of button, sew a flower center and button to each flower applique.
7. For fringe, cut four 6" x 15" strips from jeans. Matching wrong sides and long edges, press each strip in half.
8. On right side of pillow back, match folded edges of strips to edges of pillow back; baste in place.
9. With right sides together, match pillow front and back. Leaving an opening for turning and sewing through all layers, use a ¹/₄" seam allowance to sew pillow together. Remove basting threads, clip corners, and turn pillow right side out. Clip strips at ³/₄" intervals to ¹/₂" from seam. To fray fringe, wash and dry before stuffing pillow.
10. Stuff pillow with fiberfill and sew opening closed.

*F*it for a princess, our floral bedroom furniture is dreamy! A rummage-sale bed, dresser, and nightstand are painted and then accented with grid designs. To achieve the look of hand-painted roses, simply glue motifs cut from wallpaper to the furniture pieces.

BEDROOM FURNITURE

HEADBOARD

Measure the width of headboard before gathering supplies for project.

Recycled item: headboard with straight, flat top edge.

You will also need: items listed under *Preparing an Item for Painting or Decoupage* on page 157, decorative molding to fit across top of headboard, desired pieces of decorative house trim (available at home centers) in lengths to fit across top of headboard (we used two spandrel connectors for uprights and four corner brackets), drill, wood glue, clamps to hold molding and brackets in place while glue is drying, hammer, finishing nails, spray primer, desired color interior latex paint, and paintbrushes.

Allow primer, paint, and glue to dry after each application.

1. Follow *Preparing an Item for Painting or Decoupage* to prepare headboard.
2. Glue molding to front of headboard along top edge; clamp in place.
3. Mark desired position for trim pieces on top edge of headboard. Follow manufacturer's instructions to attach one spandrel connector to each end of headboard. Glue corner brackets to headboard; clamp in place. Secure trim pieces and molding with finishing nails.
4. Remove all clamps. Apply primer, then latex paint to headboard.

NIGHTSTAND

Recycled item: nightstand.
You will also need: items listed under *Preparing an Item for Painting or Decoupage* on page 157, spray primer, desired colors of interior latex paint, paintbrushes, and wallpaper.

Allow primer, paint, and glue to dry after each application.

1. Remove drawer from nightstand and knob from drawer. Follow *Preparing an Item for Painting or Decoupage* to prepare nightstand.
2. Spray nightstand, drawer, and knob with primer. Using latex paint, apply desired color for base coat to all exposed areas.
3. Paint knob, lines on top, and other areas of trim as desired.
4. Cutting to fit, follow manufacturer's instructions to apply wallpaper to front of drawer.
5. Cut desired motifs from wallpaper. Apply craft glue to wrong sides of motifs. Apply motifs to top of nightstand. Remove excess glue with a damp cloth.
6. Replace knob on drawer and drawer in nightstand.

DRESSER

Recycled item: dresser.

You will also need: items listed under *Preparing an Item for Painting or Decoupage* on 157, spray primer, desired colors of interior latex paint, paintbrushes, painter's tape, kraft paper, desired color spray paint, disposable plastic gloves, 5 mesh plastic canvas, wallpaper, and craft glue.

Allow primer, paint, and glue to dry after each application.

1. Remove drawers from dresser and knobs from drawers. Follow *Preparing an Item for Painting or Decoupage* to prepare dresser.

2. Spray dresser, drawers, and knobs with primer. Using latex paint, apply desired color for base coat to all exposed surfaces.

3. For check pattern, use painter's tape and kraft paper to mask off areas of dresser not to be painted. Wearing plastic gloves, hold plastic canvas on area to be painted. Lightly spray paint over canvas to achieve desired effect. If necessary, wash paint from plastic canvas with warm, soapy water before repositioning canvas to paint remaining areas.

4. Leaving 1" exposed along top and bottom edges, use painter's tape and kraft paper to mask off front of each drawer. Spray paint exposed areas. Paint knobs and lines on drawers as desired.

5. Cutting wallpaper pieces to fit, follow manufacturer's instructions to cover top, sides, and bottom front edge of dresser with wallpaper.

6. Cut desired motifs from wallpaper. Apply craft glue to wrong side of motifs. Apply motifs to drawer fronts as desired. Remove excess glue with a damp cloth.

7. Replace knobs on drawers and drawers in dresser.

HANDKERCHIEF FOOTSTOOL

S it back, relax, and put your feet up on our darling handkerchief footstool. While it's a perfect partner for a chair, this flowered find is a great accent all by itself! A plain wicker footstool is spray painted white and decoupaged with old floral handkerchiefs for this precious — and comfortable — creation.

DECOUPAGED FOOTSTOOL

Recycled items: footstool and three handkerchiefs.

You will also need: items listed under *Preparing an Item for Painting or Decoupage* on page 157, spray paint, decoupage sealer, and a foam brush.

Allow paint and sealer to dry after each application.

1. Follow *Preparing an Item for Painting or Decoupage* to prepare footstool.
2. Spray paint stool.
3. Matching straight edges, cut two handkerchiefs into halves.
4. Dip handkerchiefs in sealer; squeeze to remove excess sealer. Apply whole handkerchief to top of stool and one handkerchief half to each leg.
5. Follow manufacturer's instructions to apply three coats of sealer to stool.

TWIG-FRAMED MIRROR

*R*eflect a little of your creativity while "recycling" damaged dishes! Broken china pieces and twigs help create a unique frame for a small mirror. Wire-edge ribbon and a teapot lid provide a clever hanger to display your trash-to-treasure masterpiece. It's sure to get plenty of second looks!

RUSTIC TWIG MIRROR

Recycled items: corrugated cardboard, pieces of broken china, straight twigs, assorted decorative buttons, and china lid with handle for hanger.

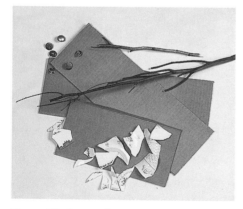

You will also need: 5" x 7" mirror, sheet moss, garden clippers to cut twigs, 30" of 1¹/₂"w wired ribbon, 28" of ⁵/₈"w wired ribbon, two 6" lengths of floral wire, and a hot glue gun.

1. Cut one 8¹/₂" x 11" and one 12" x 14" piece of cardboard. Cut a 4" x 6" opening at center of 8¹/₂" x 11" cardboard piece; glue mirror behind opening.

2. Center and glue small cardboard piece on large cardboard piece. Glue moss over exposed area of large cardboard piece.

3. Cut two each 4" and 6" twigs and four each 12" and 14¹/₂" twigs. Glue 4" and 6" twigs along edges of mirror opening. Glue two 12" and two 14¹/₂" twigs along outer edge of large cardboard. Trimming to fit and overlapping at corners, glue remaining twigs along edges of small cardboard piece.

Cutting twigs as necessary, glue twigs around mirror to cover small cardboard piece.

4. Glue china pieces and buttons over moss as desired.

5. For hanger, loop center of 1¹/₂"w ribbon around handle of china lid. Wrap floral wire around ribbon 1¹/₂" below handle to secure loop. With each end of ribbon extending beyond edge of frame, glue ribbon to back of frame; trim ends as desired. Follow *Making a Bow,* page 158, to tie ⁵/₈"w ribbon into a bow. Glue bow to hanger over floral wire. Glue button to center of bow.

TEDDY BEAR LAMP

*L*ight the way for an especially precious baby with this adorable nursery lamp. No one will ever guess that the whimsical poster board teddy bear is standing against a plastic bottle! The inventive base is filled with sand and covered with fabric, then outfitted with a lamp kit.

NURSERY LAMP

Recycled items: bottle with straight sides, lampshade, sand, and poster board.

You will also need: photocopies of bear and heart designs on page 152, wooden plaque for lamp base, three 1" dia. wooden beads, fabric to cover bottle and trim shade, acrylic paint for base and wooden beads, paintbrushes, batting, lamp kit for bottle base, colored pencils, black permanent fine-point marker, spray adhesive, and a hot glue gun.

Allow paint and glue to dry after each application. Use hot glue for all gluing unless otherwise indicated.

1. Paint plaque and beads.
2. Measure height of bottle; add 1/2". Measure around bottle. Cut a piece of batting the determined measurements. Place batting piece on wrong side of fabric and draw a line 1 1/2" outside each edge of batting. Cut out fabric piece along drawn lines. Press one long edge of fabric piece 1/2" to wrong side.
3. Apply spray adhesive to one side of batting and wrong side of fabric. Glue batting piece around bottle. With one short edge extending 1/2" beyond bottom edge of bottle and pressed edge overlapping raw edge at back of bottle, glue fabric piece around batting. Fold excess fabric to bottom of bottle and glue in place.
4. Fill bottle with sand and tuck excess fabric into opening. Follow manufacturer's instructions to attach lamp kit to bottle.

5. For trim on each edge of shade, measure around edge of shade. Cut 1"w bias strip of fabric 1" longer than edge measurement. Press each long edge and one short edge 1/4" to wrong side. With pressed edge overlapping raw edge at back of shade, glue bias strip along edge of shade.
6. Spacing evenly, glue painted beads on bottom of base. Glue base to bottom of lamp. Attach shade to lamp.
7. Follow manufacturer's instructions to fuse web to wrong side of photocopies. Fuse photocopies to poster board. Color designs as desired. Use marker to write desired message on heart on bear. Leaving a 1/8" border, cut out designs. Glue designs to bottle and shade as desired.

WALLPAPER BORDER BOXES

I f you find it difficult to draw a straight line, but you want the effect of skilled painting, these projects are just for you. Wallpaper borders offer a multitude of designs and can be pasted to almost anything in no time! Faux finishes were used to achieve the crackled, antiqued, and pickled effects on our boxes.

WALLPAPER BORDER BOXES

Allow paint, glue, gel, sealer, and wallpaper to dry after each application.

CHECKERBOARD BOX
Recycled item: wooden box with lid (we used a 20" dia. x 17"h box).
You will also need: items listed under *Preparing an Item for Painting or Decoupage* on page 157, desired colors of acrylic paint, large paintbrush, small flat paintbrush, prepasted wallpaper border, three wooden bun feet, and spray sealer.

1. Follow *Preparing an Item for Painting or Decoupage* to prepare box.
2. Paint box, lid, and feet.
3. For checkerboard, lightly draw a 12" square at center of lid. Divide 12" square into sixty-four 1½" squares.

4. Paint small squares with alternating colors. Paint a ½"w border around checkerboard. Paint border around bottom of box and edge of lid as desired. Paint accents on box and lid as desired.
5. For aged look, lightly sand painted areas; wipe clean with tack cloth. Spray box, lid, and bun feet with two or three coats of sealer.

6. Measure around box; add ½". Cut a piece of wallpaper border the determined measurement. Overlapping ends at back, follow manufacturer's instructions to apply border around box.
7. Follow manufacturer's instructions to attach feet to bottom of box.

SUNFLOWER BOX

Recycled item: wooden box with lid (we used an 11½" dia. x 5¾"h box).
You will also need: items listed under *Preparing an Item for Painting or Decoupage* on page 157, pickling gel, yellow and brown acrylic paint, paintbrush, a pencil with an unused eraser, and sunflower motif prepasted wallpaper border.

1. Follow *Preparing an Item for Painting or Decoupage* to prepare box.
2. Follow manufacturer's instructions to apply pickling gel to box and lid.
3. Use acrylic paint to paint brown circle at center of lid and yellow petals around circle.
4. Dip pencil eraser in yellow paint and paint dots on flower center.
5. Measure around box; add ½". Cut a length of wallpaper border the determined measurement. Measure around lid; add ½". Cut a piece of border to fit edge of lid. Overlapping ends at back, follow manufacturer's instructions to apply border around box and lid.

BUNNY BOX

Recycled item: wooden box (we used a 9¾"w x 9¾"d x 14"h box.)
You will also need: items listed under *Preparing an Item for Painting or Decoupage* on page 157, two colors of acrylic paint for base coat and top coat, crackle medium for acrylic paint, paintbrush, and bunny motif prepasted wallpaper border.

1. Follow *Preparing an Item for Painting or Decoupage* to prepare box.
2. Paint box with base coat. Follow crackle medium manufacturer's instructions to apply crackle medium and top coat to box.
3. For each side of box, measure width of side. Cut a piece of wallpaper border the determined measurement.
4. Follow wallpaper manufacturer's instructions to apply border pieces to box.

BROWN BAG PLACE MAT

You can set a very special place at your table with little more than two brown paper grocery sacks and some scraps of fabric! Fusible web holds this place mat together, and adhesive vinyl makes it durable. With the homestyle look of weaving and fabric appliqués, this easy creation will add a welcome touch to everyday meals.

PAPER BAG PLACE MAT

Recycled items: two large brown paper bags.

You will also need: 1¼ yds. of 18"w paper-backed fusible web, 17" x 22" piece of fabric for weaving strips, desired fabrics for appliqués, pinking shears, clothespins, and two 14" x 18" pieces of clear self-adhesive plastic.

Use straight scissors for all cutting unless otherwise indicated.

1. Cut each grocery bag open along seam, press with a dry iron.
2. For weaving strips, cut fourteen 2" x 17" strips from one bag. Fuse a 17" x 22" piece of web to wrong side of 17" x 22" piece of fabric. Use pinking shears to cut fourteen 1½" x 17" strips from fused fabric. Center and fuse one fabric strip on each paper strip.
3. For place mat backing, fuse a 12¼" x 16½" piece of web to remaining bag. Trim paper bag to edges of web.
4. Using clothespins to hold strips in place, match one short end of eight weaving strips to one long edge on web side of backing. Adjusting clothespins as necessary, weave remaining strips across place mat. Fuse strips in place and trim ends to edge of backing.
5. Using patterns, page 151, follow *Making Appliqués,* page 157, to make one flower, one center, one stem, and two leaf appliqués. Arrange appliqués on place mat, overlapping as necessary; fuse in place.
6. Remove backing from one piece of plastic. Center and smooth plastic over right side of place mat. Turn place mat to wrong side and repeat to cover back of place mat. Press plastic together around edges of place mat to insure a good seal. Leaving a ⅛" border, cut excess plastic from edges of place mat.

WALLPAPERED CANISTERS

*K*itchen canisters of a generation past — easy-to-find bargains at garage sales and flea markets — can be refurbished to fit today's decorating styles. It's a snap to paint each canister, apply a crackle finish, and then cover the container fronts with pieces of wallpaper border.

WALLPAPERED CANISTERS

Recycled item: wooden canister set.

You will also need: items listed under *Preparing an Item for Painting or Decoupage* on page 157, two colors of acrylic paint for top coat and base coat,

paintbrushes, crackle medium for acrylic paint, wallpaper border, and craft glue.

Allow paint, crackle medium, wallpaper, and glue to dry after each application.

1. Follow *Preparing an Item for Painting or Decoupage,* to prepare canisters.
2. Paint canisters with base coat. Follow manufacturer's instructions to apply crackle medium and top coat.
3. For each canister, measure area to be covered by wallpaper. Cut one piece of wallpaper the determined measurement.
4. Mix one part craft glue and one part water. Use glue mixture to apply wallpaper piece to each canister; smooth in place.

DAISY-FRESH LAMP

DAISY LAMP

*S*pring is always abloom when you make our sunny table lamp part of your home decor. To create this charming room-brightener, a large plastic soda bottle is fitted with a lamp kit and covered with warm gingham fabric. A daisy-trimmed lampshade tops it off.

Recycled items: two-liter plastic soda bottle, heavy cardboard, rubber band, lampshade, and sand or gravel to weight bottle.

You will also need: lamp kit for bottle base, fabrics to cover shade and bottle, batting, fray preventative, ribbons, silk daisies, wire cutters, four 1" dia. desired color wooden beads, and a hot glue gun.

1. Trace around bottom of bottle onto cardboard; cut out circle. Glue circle to bottom of bottle.

2. Fill bottle with sand or gravel and follow manufacturer's instructions to assemble lamp kit; do not attach cord to socket.

3. Following *Cutting a Fabric Circle,* page 157, use 18" for string measurement to cut a circle of fabric to cover bottle. Following *Cutting a Fabric Circle,* use 16" for string measurement to cut two circles of batting.

4. Center batting circles on wrong side of fabric circle. Glue center of batting to center of fabric circle. Center and glue cardboard on bottle to center of batting circle.

5. Cut a small slit in fabric near the cardboard circle large enough for cord to fit through. Apply fray preventative to raw edges of slit; allow to dry. Pull cord through slit and attach to lamp socket.

6. With cord between batting and bottle, bring edges of fabric up and gather fabric around neck of bottle. Use a rubber band to secure fabric around neck of bottle. Fold raw edges of fabric over edges of batting to wrong side and tuck under rubber band.

7. Tie several lengths of ribbon into a bow around neck of bottle.

8. To cut fabric to cover lampshade, measure around bottom edge and height of lampshade. Cut a piece of fabric twice as long as the bottom edge measurement and 1" wider than the height measurement.

9. With right sides together, use a 1/4" seam allowance to sew short edges of fabric piece together to form a tube. Turn tube right side out. Baste each edge of fabric tube 1/2" to wrong side.

10. Place fabric tube over lampshade. Pull basting thread to gather edges of fabric tube to fit edges of lampshade. Evenly distribute gathers around lampshade and glue edges of fabric to edges of lampshade. Place lampshade on lamp.

11. Cut silk daisies from stems. Glue daisies to lampshade along fabric edges. Glue one daisy to center of bow on lamp. Glue wooden beads to bottom of lamp for feet.

NECKTIE PILLOW

Trends change from year to year, and this is especially true for clothes. Before you dump all those old ties in the garage-sale box, put them together to make a stylish pillow. Just assemble the neckties in a classic quilt pattern to fashion a new accessory for your home.

VINTAGE TIE PILLOW

Recycled items: neckties (we used seven ties).

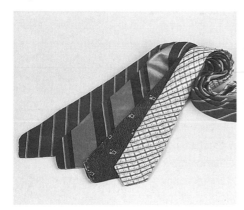

You will also need: seam ripper, tracing paper, 12" square of fabric for backing, 52" of ¹⁄₈" dia. cord, 1¹⁄₂" x 52" bias strip to make welting, polyester fiberfill, and thread.

Use ¹⁄₄" seam allowance for all sewing steps unless otherwise indicated.

1. Use seam ripper to open each tie along back seam; press open.
2. Trace patterns, page 154 and 155, onto tracing paper. Use patterns to cut one corner piece; one piece A; and two each (one in reverse) of pieces B, C, and D from ties.

3. For pillow top, matching right sides and raw edges, sew pieces A - D together (Fig. 1).

Fig. 1

4. Press curve of corner piece ¹⁄₄" to wrong side. Matching raw edges of corner piece to top left corner of pillow top, top stitch along curve close to pressed edge.
5. For welting, center cord on wrong side of bias strip. Matching long edges, fold strip over cord. Using zipper foot, machine baste along length of strip close to cord.
6. Matching raw edges and using a zipper foot, start 1" from one end of welting and baste welting to right side of backing fabric. Clip seam allowance as necessary. Remove 1" of basting from one end of welting and cut cord so that both ends of cord meet. Insert unopened end of welting in opened end. Fold raw edge of top fabric ¹⁄₂" to wrong side; baste in place.
7. Place right sides of pillow top and back together. Stitching as close to welting as possible and leaving an opening for turning and stuffing, sew pillow top and back together. Remove basting. Clipping corners as necessary, turn pillow right side out. Stuff pillow with fiberfill; sew opening closed.

WINNING LAMP

*I*deal for an office or den, this handsome lamp adds a winning touch to a gentleman's quarters. His old cup-style sports trophy and a painted plaque provide the base for this light, which is topped with a dandy lampshade covered with outdated neckties.

"TIED" TROPHY LAMP

Recycled items: cup-style trophy, neckties, and a lampshade.

You will also need: candle lamp, plaque for lamp base, acrylic paint for base, paintbrush, flat trim, household cement, and a hot glue gun.

Allow paint and glue to dry after each application. Use hot glue for all gluing unless otherwise indicated.

1. For base, paint plaque.
2. Use household cement to glue candle lamp into trophy.
3. Measure side of shade from top to bottom. Cut a piece from large end of each tie 1½" longer than determined measurement.

4. With tie points extending past bottom edge of shade and side edges overlapping slightly, glue tie pieces around shade. Trim tie pieces even with top edge of shade.
5. Cut a length of trim to fit around top edge of shade; glue in place. Glue base to bottom of trophy and attach shade.

Fun FIX-UPS

*F*inding a new use for discards can be simple and fun when you use this collection of ideas as a guide. Our fast and exciting projects will get everyone (even kids!) involved in creative recycling. Make festive birthday party favors from cardboard tubes, or create fanciful furniture for a special little girl's doll house. Versatile baskets are cleverly fashioned from shoe boxes, while colorful cushions stuffed with plastic grocery bags make a comfortable way to dress up outdoor chairs. With so many easy-to-do projects, the only difficult step is deciding where to begin!

COTTAGE BOOKENDS

BOOKEND HOUSES

Add a homey touch to your favorite collection of stories with our creative paper carton bookends. These accents are so charming, they'll make your books look right at home! Wooden craft sticks provide "shingled" rooftops for the fabric-covered cottages.

Recycled items: 1-pint carton or 1¼-pint carton, sand, fabric scraps, felt scraps, and buttons.

For each house, you will also need: desired color acrylic paint, paintbrush, tracing paper, transfer paper, ten jumbo craft sticks, craft scissors, pinking shears, raffia tied into a small bow, brown marker, dried greenery, spray adhesive, and a hot glue gun.

Use hot glue for all gluing unless otherwise indicated.

1. Carefully open carton and fill with sand; reseal with hot glue.
2. Paint carton; allow to dry.
3. Cut a 2" square of fabric. Cut fabric square in half diagonally. Use spray adhesive to apply one half to each indentation on roof (Fig. 1).

Fig. 1

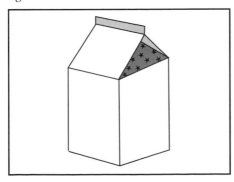

4. To cover ridge of roof, cut a 1½" x 3" fabric piece. Use spray adhesive to apply fabric piece.
5. Cut a 5" x 12" fabric piece. Apply spray adhesive to wrong side of fabric. Matching one long edge of fabric to top side edges and overlapping ends at one corner, glue fabric around carton. Fold excess fabric to bottom; glue to secure.
6. Trace shingle pattern, page 149, onto tracing paper. Use transfer paper to transfer pattern onto craft sticks for sixteen shingles. Use craft scissors to cut shingles from craft sticks. With ends of shingles extending past edge of carton, glue bottom row of shingles on each side of roof. Cut two shingles in half lengthwise. Staggering placement with bottom row, overlap and glue top row of shingles to each side of roof. Glue a button to front and back of roof.
7. For each side window, use pinking shears to cut a 1½" x 2" piece from felt. Cut a ¾" x 1⅛" piece from craft stick; glue to center of felt piece. Use marker to draw panes on window. Center and glue window to side of carton.
8. For door, cut one craft stick in half. Use marker to draw window on door. Glue door to felt. Leaving a ¼"w felt border, use pinking shears to cut around door. Using craft scissors, trim felt even with bottom of door. Glue door to front of house and button to door for door handle.
9. For window over door, use pinking shears to cut a 1¼" x 1½" piece from felt. Cut a ⅝" x ¾" piece from craft stick; glue to center of felt piece. Use marker to draw panes on window. Center and glue window above door.
10. Glue raffia bow above door. Glue greenery to house as desired.
11. If desired, cut a piece of felt slightly smaller than bottom of house; glue in place.

RECYCLER'S CUSHION

*D*ress up any casual chair with a comfy cushion. Stuffed with "recycled" plastic bags, this seat pad makes great use of those shopping bags that accumulate so quickly. Choose a fabric that complements your patio furniture, or select a novelty print to coordinate with the season.

CHAIR CUSHION

Recycled items: plastic bags and a paper grocery bag.

You will also need: vinyl-coated fabric.

1. Place paper bag on chair seat; draw around seat. Cut out 2" outside drawn line to make pattern. Mark location of chair uprights on pattern for tie placements.
2. Fold fabric in half; pin pattern to fabric. Cut around pattern through both fabric layers. Mark tie placements on right side of one fabric piece.
3. For each tie, cut a 1½" x 24" strip of fabric. Press each edge of strip ¼" to wrong side. Matching long edges and wrong sides, press strip in half. Stitching close to pressed edges, sew along length of strip. Fold tie in half and baste fold to placement mark at edge of fabric piece (Fig 1).

Fig. 1

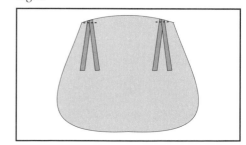

4. Place right sides of fabric pieces together. Leaving an opening between ties for turning, use a ½" seam allowance to sew fabric pieces together. Clip seam allowance and turn right side out. Stuff cushion with plastic bags. Leaving three 1" openings for air vents, sew opening closed.

STEP STOOL PLANT STAND

*G*ive your plants a "step up" with a colorfully painted step stool! This exciting project is a great way to make use of that old stool and battered clay pots taking up space in your garage or storage building. Using simple floral designs trimmed in grid lines, polka dots, and stripes, you can create a cheery way to show off your leafy green friends!

FLOWERPOTS AND STAND

Recycled items: clay flowerpots and a wooden step stool.

You will also need: items listed under *Preparing an Item for Painting or Decoupage* on page 157, spray primer, white spray paint, tracing paper, transfer paper, black and green acrylic paint, desired colors of acrylic paint, paintbrushes, pencil with unused eraser, and clear spray sealer.

Allow primer, paint, and sealer to dry after each application.

1. Follow *Preparing an Item for Painting or Decoupage* to prepare flowerpots and step stool.
2. Spray flowerpots and step stool with primer. Apply two coats of white spray paint. Use desired acrylic paints to paint rungs and front edges of steps.
3. For flowers, use acrylic paints to paint 1³/₄" dia. circles on flowerpots and step stool as desired. To add leaves, trace Blue Jean Pillow Leaf pattern, page 143, onto tracing paper. Use transfer paper to transfer leaves around flower designs.
4. Use black paint to outline flowers and leaves, paint swirls on flowers, and paint veins on leaves.
5. Using desired color paints, paint stripe and plaid designs on flowerpots and plant stand. Use pencil eraser to paint dots.
6. Spray flowerpots and plant stand with two coats of sealer.

PERKY PICNIC BASKET

PICNIC BASKET

*P*ut the life back into a tired metal picnic basket with motifs cut from a perky floral print fabric! Using fabric, rickrack, and acrylic paints, you can create an eye-catching carrier for toting food for any occasion. This neat basket also makes a cheerful kitchen decoration.

Recycled item: metal picnic basket with handles.

You will also need: items listed under *Preparing an Item for Painting or Decoupage* on page 157, 1"w masking tape, white spray paint, pencil, ruler, flower motif fabric, green acrylic paint for stems and assorted colors of acrylic paint to coordinate with fabric, paintbrushes, tracing paper, compressed craft sponge, paper towels, craft knife, acrylic spray sealer, cardboard, batting, jumbo rickrack, fabric glue, and a hot glue gun.

Allow paint, sealer, and glue to dry after each application. Use hot glue for all gluing unless otherwise indicated.

1. Follow *Preparing an Item for Painting or Decoupage* to prepare basket. Cover handles with masking tape if desired.
2. Spray paint basket white.
3. With bottom edge of tape 1/8" above bottom edge of basket, apply one strip of masking tape around bottom of basket. Leaving a 1/8" space between strips of tape, apply a second strip of masking tape around basket (Fig. 1).

Fig. 1

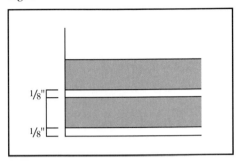

4. Using desired colors, paint area between tape strips and area below tape.
5. Remove masking tape from handles and around basket. Cut a 1/2" square from sponge. Follow *Compressed Sponge Painting,* page 159, to paint check pattern around basket between painted lines.
6. Cut flower motifs from fabric. Use fabric glue to glue flowers to sides of basket as desired.
7. For leaves, trace leaf pattern, page 148, onto tracing paper; cut out. Draw around pattern on sponge; cut out. Use sponge to paint leaves as desired. Using green paint, paint a stem below each flower.
8. Spray basket with two to three coats of sealer.
9. To pad lid, draw around basket lid on cardboard. Cut out cardboard 1/4" inside drawn line. Draw around cardboard on batting and wrong side of fabric. Cut out batting along drawn line. Cut out fabric 1" outside drawn line. Clip edges of fabric to 1/4" from drawn line. Glue batting to cardboard. Center fabric over batting and glue fabric edges to back of cardboard. With half of rickrack extending beyond edge of fabric-covered cardboard, glue rickrack to back of cardboard. Glue cardboard to top of basket.

*A*dorable juice can babies are an amusing way to welcome a new arrival to the world! The cute aluminum characters are diapered with felt and crowned with wisps of curly doll hair. You can use them to trim a shower tree centerpiece or a welcome-home wreath (shown on page 108). Our easy baby bottle favors, made from toilet paper tubes covered in nursery fabric and filled with treats, are perfect for sharing with well-wishers.

BABY SHOWER DECORATIONS

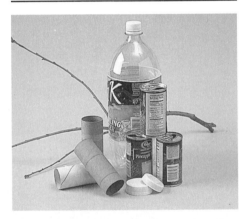

Allow primer, paint, and glue to dry after each application.

CAN BABY ORNAMENT
Recycled items: six-ounce beverage can and scrap of white paper.
You will also need: spray primer, flesh-color spray paint; white, pink, and blue acrylic paint; small paintbrushes; 5¹/₄" square of white felt; 5mm pink pom-pom; two ³/₄" brass safety pins; curly doll hair; black permanent fine-point marker; and a hot glue gun.

1. For each baby ornament, remove tab from can. Use both hands to hold can with thumbs below top rim and opening. Using thumbs, press on can to bend top rim down (Fig. 1). Turn can upside down and repeat to bend bottom of can in opposite direction. Step on can to flatten further.

Fig. 1

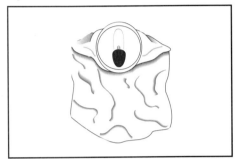

2. Spray can with primer, then flesh paint. Using pink paint, paint cheeks and inside mouth.
3. Use marker to draw eyes and eyelashes on face. Paint eyes blue; paint whites of eyes and add a sparkle of white to blue eyes.
4. If tooth is desired, cut a ¹/₈" x ¹/₂" piece of white paper. Leaving ¹/₈" of paper piece showing, center and glue piece inside mouth.
5. Center and glue pom-pom above mouth for nose. Glue doll hair to top of can as desired.
6. For diaper, fold felt square diaper-style around bottom of can; glue in place. Pin safety pins to front of diaper.

BABY BOTTLE FAVOR
Recycled items: toilet paper tube and a 1¹/₂" dia. white plastic lid.
You will also need: 5¹/₂" x 8" piece of white fabric, 4" white chenille stem, candy or other items to fill favor, baby bottle nipple, spray adhesive and thick craft glue.

1. Spray toilet paper tube with adhesive. With excess fabric extending ¹/₂" at one end of tube, center tube on wrong side of fabric; glue around tube. Smooth ¹/₂" edge of excess fabric over edge and glue inside tube. Twist chenille stem around excess fabric at remaining end of tube and stuff inside tube.
2. Fill tube with desired items and glue plastic lid to open end of tube. Glue a nipple to lid.
3. Tie lengths of ribbon into a bow around bottle as desired.

TABLETOP TREE DECORATION
Recycled items: two-liter plastic soda bottle, sand to weight bottle, and a small tree branch approximately 32" long.
You will also need: desired number of Can Baby Ornaments and Baby Bottle Favors, white spray paint, receiving blanket, assorted baby items (we used baby shoes, baby socks, pacifiers, diaper pins, and a comb and brush set), assorted ribbons, paper clips, and a hot glue gun.

1. For hanger on each baby or bottle, unfold one paper clip and glue one end to back of baby or bottle.
2. Trim branch into desired shape; spray paint.
3. Fill soda bottle half full with sand. Insert base of branch into bottle, pushing firmly into sand.
4. Center soda bottle on wrong side of receiving blanket. Gathering blanket around neck of bottle, tie several lengths of ribbon into a bow to secure. Pin a diaper pin to center of bow.
5. Place Can Baby Ornaments and Bottle Favors on tree. Attach a diaper pin to each sock. Use ribbon to attach each baby item to tree as desired.

WREATH

Recycled item: desired wreath (we used a heart-shaped grapevine wreath).

You will also need: desired number of Can Baby Ornaments, white spray paint, small artificial flowers, desired colors of infant socks, pacifiers, assorted ribbons, white chenille stem, and a hot glue gun.

1. Spray paint wreath.
2. For sock bouquet, tie desired ribbon lengths into a bow around a small stack of socks just below the cuffs. Thread chenille stem through ribbon at back of sock bouquet. Use chenille stem to secure sock bouquet to wreath as desired.

3. Arrange and glue flowers and Can Baby Ornaments to wreath as desired.
4. To attach each pacifier, thread lengths of ribbon through a twig on wreath and tie ends of ribbon into a bow through pacifier ring.

WORKOUT PARTNERS

*Y*ou'll arrive at the gym in personalized style with this handy carry-all! Choose a canvas tote that's roomy enough for all your workout gear and embellish it with a design from an old T-shirt. You can use leftover shirt material and abandoned buttons to put together a quick hair scrunchie to complete this exercise ensemble.

TOTE AND SCRUNCHIE

Recycled items: T-shirt with desired design and assorted buttons.

You will also need: canvas bag to fit design from T-shirt, 15" square of paper-backed fusible web, flat trim, 6" of ¼"w elastic, shoestrings, embroidery floss, and fabric glue.

TOTE BAG

1. Turn T-shirt inside out; press. Following manufacturer's instructions, center and fuse web to wrong side of design. Turn shirt right side out. Cut around design as desired; remove paper backing. Center and fuse design to one side of bag.

2. Glue trim over edges of design; allow to dry.
3. Tie shoestrings into a bow around handle. Glue buttons to front of bag as desired; allow to dry.

SCRUNCHIE

1. Cut a 3" x 23" strip from T-shirt fabric. Matching wrong sides and long edges, fold strip in half. Using a ¼" seam allowance,

sew long edges together to form a tube.
2. Turn tube right side out. Use floss to sew buttons to tube.
3. Thread elastic through center of tube. Overlap ends of elastic ½" and sew together. At one end, turn edge ½" to inside of tube. Insert raw end of tube inside turned end; stitch ends together.

NEWSPAPER VEGGIES

*P*ick your own peck of
paper produce! These newspaper
veggies not only look realistic, but
they're also very easy to make.
Sponge-painted newspaper pieces
are simply formed into vegetable
shapes. You'll have a harvest of
garden beauties in no time!

NEWSPAPER VEGGIES

Allow paint, sealer, and glue to dry after
each application. Use craft glue for all
projects unless otherwise indicated. When
sponge painting, work from lightest to
darkest color unless otherwise indicated.

Recycled item: newspaper.
You will also need: aluminum foil, natural
sponge pieces, craft glue, and a hot glue gun.
For green onions, you will also need:
cream and green acrylic paint, glossy spray
sealer, jute twine, and raffia.
For carrots, you will also need: three
colors of orange acrylic paint, three colors
of green acrylic paint, jute twine, and raffia.
For radishes, you will also need: red, dark
red, and green acrylic paint; ecru
embroidery floss; and raffia.
For peppers, you will also need: yellow,
orange, red, and dark red acrylic paint;
paintbrush; glossy spray sealer; and twigs.
For peas, you will also need: tracing paper;
light green, green, and bright green acrylic

paint; green floral wire; pencil; and spray
adhesive.
For cabbage, you will also need: four
colors of green acrylic paint and a pencil.
For potatoes, you will also need: white,
black, and four different colors of brown
acrylic paint.

GREEN ONIONS
1. Cut two 12" squares from newspaper.
Paint one square cream for onion bottoms
and remaining square green for onion tops.
Spray green square with sealer.
2. For each onion, shape a piece of foil into
a 2" long teardrop.
3. For each onion top, cut a 1" x 10" piece
from green square. Fold one long edge ¼"
to wrong side. Matching folded edge to

remaining long edge, fold and glue piece in half. Hot glue one end of onion top to pointed end of foil shape. Pinch onion top to shape as desired. Repeat to add desired number of tops.

4. Tear a piece of paper from cream square large enough to cover foil shape. Covering base of onion tops and folding paper over ends as necessary, glue paper piece around foil shape.

5. For roots, cut 3" of twine. Hot glue one end of twine to bottom of onion; unravel.

6. If desired, use raffia to tie several onions together.

CARROTS

1. For each carrot, cut a 5" x 11" piece from newspaper. Divide newspaper piece into two painting sections by drawing a line across paper 5" from one short edge.

2. Working from darkest to lightest color, follow *Sponge Painting*, page 159, to paint large section orange on one side and small section green on both sides.

3. For carrot top, make tears 1/4" apart from top edge of green section to orange section.

4. Shape a piece of unpainted newspaper into a 6" long carrot. Wrap a piece of foil around newspaper shape.

5. For roots, cut 4" of twine. Hot glue one end of twine to point of carrot shape; unravel.

6. With green section of newspaper extending past large end, glue orange section of paper piece around carrot shape.

7. Pinch base of carrot top section together; glue to secure.

8. If desired, use raffia to tie several carrots together.

RADISHES

1. Cut two 12" squares of newspaper.

2. Following *Sponge Painting*, page 159, paint one side of one square red and both sides of remaining square green.

3. For each radish, shape a piece of unpainted newspaper into a 1" dia. ball. Wrap a piece of foil around newspaper ball.

4. Cut a piece from red square large enough to cover ball; glue around ball.

5. For roots, cut 6" of floss. Fold floss in half, hot glue fold to bottom of radish, and separate strands.

6. For leaves, tear a 1" x 6" strip from green square. Fold strip in half; hot glue fold to top of radish.

7. If desired, use raffia to tie several radishes together.

PEPPERS

1. For each pepper, cut a 12" square from newspaper and a 1" twig.

2. Following *Sponge Painting*, page 159, paint one side of square and twig red.

3. Shape a piece of unpainted newspaper into a 3" x 5" pepper shape. Wrap a piece of foil around shape.

4. Cutting away excess paper as necessary, glue painted paper around pepper shape. Hot glue twig to top of pepper for stem.

5. Use yellow and orange paint to highlight pepper. Spray lightly with sealer.

PEAS

1. Cut two 12" squares from newspaper. Working from darkest to lightest color, follow *Sponge Painting*, page 159, to paint one side of each square green.

2. Trace pea pod pattern, page 151, onto tracing paper; cut out.

3. For each pea, use pattern to cut two pieces from painted newspaper. Shape a piece of foil into a 5" long curve. Glue foil shape to wrong side of one pea pod piece. Use a thin line of hot glue to glue edges of pea pod pieces together around foil piece. Pinch pea pod to shape peas as desired.

4. Thread desired number of pea pods onto an 18" length of floral wire. Spacing 1" apart; glue in place. Curl each end of floral wire around pencil.

CABBAGE

1. Following *Sponge Painting*, page 159, paint both sides of one sheet of newspaper and one side of a second sheet of newspaper green.

2. For cabbage center, shape a piece of unpainted newspaper into a 4" dia. ball. Wrap a piece of foil around newspaper ball. Smooth and slightly flatten one side of ball for bottom of cabbage.

3. Cut a piece from newspaper painted on one side large enough to cover ball; glue around ball.

4. For leaves, roughly tear four 5" squares and three 7" squares from remaining sheet.

5. Beginning with 5" squares and overlapping slightly, glue one corner of each square to bottom of cabbage. Curl loose edges of leaves outward by wrapping around a pencil (Fig. 1).

Fig. 1

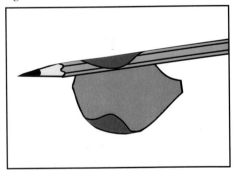

POTATOES

1. For each potato, cut a 10" square from newspaper.

2. Following *Sponge Painting*, page 159, paint one side of square brown.

3. Shape a piece of unpainted newspaper into a 2" x 4" potato shape. Wrap a piece of foil around shape.

4. Cutting away excess paper as necessary, glue painted newspaper square around potato shape.

5. Use black paint to shade and white paint to highlight potato.

BIRTHDAY PARTY FAVORS

BIRTHDAY CANDLE FAVORS

What birthday party would be complete without candles! Made from bathroom tissue tubes, these easy-to-make favors will be the hit of the celebration. Party guests are sure to have big smiles on their faces when they carry home your handmade containers filled with goodies!

SMALL FAVORS

Recycled items: toilet paper tubes.
For each small favor, you will also need: 6" x 10" piece of fabric, 6" of flat lace trim, two 6" lengths of chenille stem, 2" triangle of orange tissue paper, 2¹/₂" triangle of yellow tissue paper, ³/₈"w ribbon tied into a bow, candy to fill favor, spray adhesive, and thick craft glue.

Allow glue to dry after each application. Use craft glue for all gluing unless otherwise indicated.

1. Spray outside of tube with spray adhesive. With fabric extending at ends of tube, center and glue fabric around tube.
2. Using one length of chenille stem, gather and secure fabric at bottom of tube; stuff into tube. Fill tube with candy.
3. For wick, gather and secure fabric at top of tube with remaining chenille stem. Center orange triangle on yellow triangle. Pinch bottom edges of triangles together; glue to wick.
4. Glue lace around bottom edge of favor and bow to top edge of favor.

LARGE FAVORS

Recycled items: round containers.
For each large favor, you will also need: desired fabric, curling ribbon, flat lace trim, 6" of chenille stem, 2" triangle of orange tissue paper, 2¹/₂" triangle of yellow tissue paper, desired items to fill container, curling ribbon, spray adhesive, and thick craft glue.

Allow glue to dry after each application. Use craft glue for all gluing unless otherwise indicated.

1. Measure around container; add 1". Measure height of container; add 4". Cut a piece of fabric the determined measurements.
2. Spray outside of container with spray adhesive. With excess fabric extending beyond top edge of container, glue fabric around container. Fill container as desired.
3. For wick, gather and secure fabric at top of tube with chenille stem. Center orange triangle on yellow triangle. Pinch bottom edges of triangles together; glue to wick.
4. Glue lace around bottom edge of favor. Tie curling ribbon around wick.

CLOWN TRAIN

*S*end in the clowns for your child's next birthday bash! Our delightful toilet paper tube characters have hopped a train constructed from gourmet coffee tins and a cardboard canister. Great for boys or girls, this fun project is sure to catch the eye of all the party-goers!

CLOWN FAVORS

Recycled items: toilet paper tubes.
For each favor, you will also need:
6" x 8" piece of fabric, tracing paper, color poster board for hat, foil baking cup liner, 2½" dia. foam ball, two 2" lengths of red chenille stems, four assorted pom-poms, star stickers, two 12mm wiggle eyes, candy to fill favor, curling ribbon, spray adhesive, and a hot glue gun.

Allow glue to dry after each application. Use hot glue for all gluing unless otherwise indicated.

1. Spray outside of tube with spray adhesive. With excess fabric extending beyond bottom of tube, glue fabric around tube.
2. With shiny side up, center and glue foil liner over top of tube. Center and glue foam ball to foil liner. For hair, cut and curl several lengths of curling ribbon; glue to top of ball.
3. For hat, trace pattern, page 148, onto tracing paper; cut out. Use pattern to cut hat from poster board. Overlap straight edges ½" and glue to secure. Glue hat to head. Glue stars and pom-pom to hat.
4. Bend one chenille stem into a smile for mouth. Glue mouth, pom-pom for nose, and wiggle eyes to ball for face. Glue remaining pom-poms to front of clown as desired.

5. Fill tube with candy. Gather excess fabric at end of tube with remaining piece of chenille stem; stuff into tube.

TRAIN

Recycled items: small round can with lid for engine, rectangular cans for cars, large buttons for wheels, and a spool for smoke stack.
You will also need: desired fabric, desired colors of acrylic paint, paintbrushes, foil baking cup liner, dome-shaped button, 6" of black bump chenille stem, ¼"w ribbon, curling ribbon, spray adhesive, and a hot glue gun.

Allow paint and glue to dry after each application. Use hot glue for all gluing unless otherwise indicated.

1. Paint lid and bottom of round can, rectangular cans, and spool desired colors.
2. For engine, measure around can; add 1". Measure height of can. Cut a piece of fabric the determined measurements. Spray wrong side of fabric with spray adhesive. Overlapping ends, glue fabric around can. Replace lid on can.
3. Glue spool to side of can opposite fabric overlap. Glue end of chenille stem into center of spool; shape as desired. Glue four buttons to engine for wheels. Flatten and fold foil liner into fourths. Glue folded point of foil liner to center of lid. Center and glue dome-shaped button over point of foil liner. Center and glue one end of a 10" length of ¼"w ribbon to bottom edge at back of engine.
4. For each car, glue four buttons to painted tin for wheels. Center and glue a 10" length of ¼"w ribbon to bottom edge of car at each end.
5. To connect cars and engine, tie ribbons into bows. Fill cars with clowns and curling ribbon as desired.

VINTAGE SILVERWARE FRAMES

*O*dd silverware pieces become excellent flea market finds when used to create distinctive picture frames. Bend them back, glue them on, or arrange them in a silver creamer — the possibilities for these simple projects are endless!

SILVERWARE FRAMES

Recycled items: silver spoon with large flat handle for Spoon Frame; silver spoons and silver creamer for Creamer Frame; or silver flatware, wooden frame, and corsage pin for Silverware Frame.

You will also need: photocopies of desired photographs, desired ribbon, craft glue, and a hot glue gun.

For spoon frame, you will also need: silver cord and a ribbon rose.

For creamer frame, you will also need: floral foam, silver cord, ribbon roses, and Spanish moss.

For silverware frame, you will also need: desired color of spray paint, whitewash spray paint, sandpaper, flat lace, 1¼" wooden ball knob, and desired silver beads.

Use hot glue for all steps, unless otherwise indicated. Allow paint and glue to dry after each application.

SPOON FRAME

1. Bend spoon handle to desired angle. Trim photocopy to fit in spoon. Use craft glue to glue in place.
2. Beginning and ending at bottom of photo, glue cord around photo. Glue ribbon rose over ends of cord.
3. Tie ribbons together into a bow around handle; glue in place.

CREAMER FRAME

1. Trim foam to fit inside creamer; glue in place.
2. Trim a photocopy to fit in each spoon. Use craft glue to glue in place.
3. Beginning and ending at bottom of photos, glue cord around each photo. Glue one ribbon rose over ends of cord on each spoon.
4. Insert spoon handles into foam. Glue moss over foam.
5. Tie cord and ribbon into a bow around handle of center spoon. Knot ends of cord. Glue a ribbon rose to knot of bow.

SILVERWARE FRAME

1. Paint frame and wooden knob with spray paint, then with whitewash. For aged look, lightly sand knob and edges of frame.
2. Glue knob hole-side-up to top of frame.

Glue flatware to front of frame. Glue lace to sides of frame.

3. Thread beads onto pin. Insert and glue pin in hole of knob. Tie ribbon into a bow around pin.
4. For stand, bend two forks to desired angle; glue handles to back of frame (Fig. 1).

Fig. 1

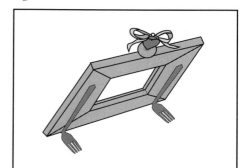

RECYCLED BAG KEEPER

*O*ur hanging keeper will
organize those plastic grocery bags
and keep them handy for jobs
around the house. Fashioned from
a plastic three-liter soda bottle and
a piece of fabric, this tidy home
helper is a friend to our
environment!

PLASTIC BAG KEEPER

Recycled items: three-liter soda bottle and
a plastic bag for hanger.

You will also need: photocopy of "recycle"
design on page 153, 6¹/₄" x 17" piece of
colored paper, 13¹/₄" x 17" piece of fabric,
6" of ¹/₄"w elastic, decorative-edge scissors,
colored markers, hole punch, and craft glue.

Allow glue to dry after each application.

1. For elastic casing, press one short edge
of fabric piece ³/₄" to wrong side. Sew along
fabric ¹/₂" from turned edge. Thread elastic
through casing; tack elastic ends at each
end of casing.
2. Matching right sides and long edges, use
a ¹/₄" seam allowance to sew long edges
together; turn right side out.

3. Cut a 6¹/₂" tube from center section of
soda bottle. Overlap and glue raw edge of
fabric around one edge of plastic tube.
4. Use markers to color photocopy; cut out.
Trim edges of colored paper with
decorative-edge scissors. Center and glue
photocopy on colored paper. Overlapping
ends at back and covering raw edge of

fabric, glue paper around plastic tube.
5. For hanger, punch a hole ³/₄" below top
edge on opposite sides of bag keeper. Cut
three 2" x 12" strips from plastic bag. Knot
strips together at one end. With knot inside,
thread strips through one hole. Tightly braid
strips and thread ends through remaining
hole; knot to secure.

SHOE BOX BASKETS

A tisket, a tasket, a quick and simple basket! Shoe boxes make great storage spots for a variety of notions, but you need not keep them out of sight. Covered in fabric or paper and finished with handles, the baskets become as decorative as they are useful.

SHOE BOX BASKETS

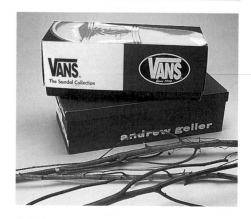

"MY GARDEN" BOX

Recycled items: shoe box, heavy cardboard, brown paper bags, twigs, and items to decorate box (we used fabric, ribbon, paper, and buttons).

You will also need: spray varnish, four 12" lengths of black craft wire, garden clippers, nail, desired color permanent marker, spray adhesive, craft glue, and a hot glue gun.

Allow paint, varnish, and glue to dry after each application. Use hot glue for all gluing unless otherwise indicated.

1. To reinforce bottom of box, cut a piece of cardboard the same size as bottom of box; glue in place.
2. Cut paper bag open along back seam;

press flat. Following *Covering a Box,* page 156, use spray adhesive to cover box with paper bag; spray with varnish if desired.

3. Measuring from bottom of box, cut two twigs desired height for handle. Center and glue twigs inside ends of box. Cut a twig slightly longer than box; glue to top of side twigs. Wrap a length of wire around each corner of handle to secure.
4. At each end of box, use nail to make two holes on each side of handle. Reinforce handle by inserting a length of wire through holes to form an "x". Twist wire ends on inside of box to secure. Tear a 2" x 18" strip of fabric and tie into a bow; glue to handle.
5. Tear one piece of fabric 1/2" smaller than long side of box. Tear a second piece of fabric 1/2" shorter and 2 1/2" narrower than first piece of fabric. Tear a piece of brown paper 1/4" shorter and 1 1/4" narrower than second piece of fabric. Use marker to write "My Garden" on paper piece. Beginning

with largest piece of fabric and using craft glue, center and glue fabric pieces, then paper piece to side of box. Glue narrow ribbon between fabric and edges of box. Glue buttons to bow and basket as desired.

PRODUCE BOX

Recycled items: shoe box, heavy cardboard, and twigs.

You will also need: desired paper to cover box, spray varnish, four 12" lengths of black craft wire, raffia, garden clippers, nail, spray adhesive, and a hot glue gun.

Allow paint, varnish, and glue to dry after each application. Use hot glue for all gluing unless otherwise indicated.

1. Using desired paper, follow Steps 1 - 5 of "My Garden" Box to cover box and add handle.
2. Cutting to fit, glue twigs along outer edges and corners of box. Tie several lengths of raffia into a bow around handle.

RECIPES BOX

Recycled items: shoe box, heavy cardboard, and items to decorate box (we used fabric and paper).

You will also need: desired paper to cover box, spray varnish, two 12" lengths of black craft wire, raffia, nail, pinking shears, 1¹/₂" x 11" piece of heavy off-white paper, desired color permanent felt-tip marker, craft glue, spray adhesive, and a hot glue gun.

Allow paint, varnish, and glue to dry after each application. Use hot glue for all gluing unless otherwise indicated.

1. For divider, cut a piece of cardboard same size as end of box. If necessary, trim cardboard to fit inside box.
2. To reinforce bottom of box, cut a piece of cardboard the same size as bottom of box; glue in place.
3. Following *Covering a Box,* page 156, use spray adhesive to cover box and divider with desired paper; spray with varnish if desired.

4. Braid raffia to desired length for handle. Knot a length of raffia around each end of braid to secure. Glue ends of braid to outside of box.
5. At each end of box, use nail to make two holes on each side of handle. Reinforce handle by inserting a length of wire through holes to form an "x". Twist wire ends on inside of box to secure.
6. Use pinking shears to cut seven 2" x 2¹/₄" pieces from assorted fabric scraps. Spacing letters 1" apart, use marker to write "RECIPES" on off-white paper; cut letters apart. Use craft glue to glue fabric pieces to front of box as desired. Using craft glue, center and glue one letter to each fabric piece to spell "RECIPES." Tear two 2" x 18" strips of fabric and tie each into a bow. Glue one bow to each side of handle.

DARLING DOLL DECOR

*L*ittle girls know that dolls need a place to call home, too! These quaint furniture pieces and accessories will furnish any dollhouse with style. Constructed from cardboard salt containers and a cigar box, our tailor-made bedroom furnishings can be covered in any fabric to fit the taste of a happy young homemaker.

DOLL FURNITURE

Recycled items: lightweight cardboard, cigar box for bed, one salt container and one toilet paper tube for each chair, and lid from mouthwash bottle and $1^{1}/_{4}$" dia. plastic lid for lamp.

You will also need: tracing paper, desired fabrics, batting, polyester fiberfill, desired colors of acrylic paint, paintbrushes, compass, craft knife, two colors of pre-gathered trim and 1"w single fold bias tape for bed, 7" of $^{1}/_{4}$" dia. wooden dowel and two large wooden beads with $^{1}/_{4}$" dia. holes for lamp, and a hot glue gun.

Allow paint to dry after each application. Use a $^{1}/_{4}$" seam allowance for all stitching.

BED

1. For bedding pattern, draw around bottom of box on tracing paper. Cut out tracing paper $1^{1}/_{4}$" outside drawn line.
2. For bed, glue cigar box closed; paint as desired. Leaving one short end uncovered and turning raw end to wrong side, glue pre-gathered trims around box for bedskirt.
3. For comforter, use bedding pattern to cut two pieces from desired fabrics and one piece from batting. Matching right sides and leaving an opening for stuffing and turning, sew fabric pieces together; turn right side out. Cut away $^{1}/_{4}$" along all edges of batting piece. Place batting piece between joined fabric pieces; smooth in place. Sew opening closed. Work *Running Stitch*, page 159, 1" inside edges around comforter.
4. For mattress, trim bedding pattern $^{3}/_{4}$" inside all edges. Use pattern to cut two pieces from desired fabric and two pieces from batting. Matching right sides and leaving an opening for stuffing and turning, sew fabric pieces together; turn right side out. Cut away $^{1}/_{4}$" along all edges of batting pieces. Place batting pieces between joined fabric pieces; smooth in place. Sew opening closed.
5. For headboard, use compass to draw a curve across one short edge of bedding pattern; trim pattern along curved line. Cut $1^{1}/_{4}$" from remaining short edge of pattern. Use pattern to cut two pieces from desired fabric and three pieces from cardboard.
6. Matching edges, stack two cardboard pieces; glue to secure. For headboard trim piece, draw a line 1" inside curved edge and long edges on remaining cardboard piece. Cut out along drawn line; discard center piece.
7. Draw around inside edge of headboard trim piece on batting; cut out. Center and glue batting piece on headboard.
8. Center one fabric piece over batting on headboard. Trimming as necessary, glue fabric edges to headboard around batting. Center headboard, fabric-covered side up, on wrong side of remaining fabric piece. Folding over edges of headboard; glue fabric edges to front of headboard.
9. Trace around headboard trim piece on batting; cut out. Glue batting to trim piece. Beginning at one end and gluing as necessary, wrap bias tape around trim piece.
10. Matching curved edges, glue trim piece to front of headboard. Glue headboard to end of bed.
11. For each large pillow, cut two 3" x 4" pieces from fabric. With right sides together and leaving an opening for turning, sew pieces together. Turn right side out and stuff with fiberfill; sew opening closed. Repeat using two 2" or two $2^{1}/_{2}$" squares of fabric for small pillows.
12. Place mattress, comforter, and pillows on bed.

CHAIRS

1. Following *Making Patterns,* page 156, use tracing paper to make chair pattern, page 150; cut out.
2. Matching bottom edge of pattern to bottom edge of container; draw around chair pattern on back of salt container. Draw a line around front of container between side edges of chair pattern $2^{1}/_{2}$" above bottom edge. Cut out chair along drawn lines.
3. Cutting 1" outside edges of pattern, use chair pattern to cut one piece each from fabric and batting. Cut a $3^{1}/_{2}$" x 8" piece from fabric and a $2^{1}/_{2}$" x 6" piece from batting.
4. Matching bottom edges of batting pieces to bottom edge of chair; glue batting pieces around outside of chair. Folding long edges of fabric over edges of batting and chair, center and glue $3^{1}/_{2}$" x 8" fabric piece over batting on front of chair. Folding side edges of fabric to wrong side and remaining edges over edges of chair, center and glue remaining fabric piece over batting on back of chair.
5. For inside chair back, draw around chair pattern on cardboard; cut out $^{1}/_{4}$" inside drawn lines. Cut two 3" circles from cardboard.
6. Draw around each cardboard piece on wrong side of fabric; cut out 1" outside drawn lines. Cut a 3" circle from batting. Center and glue batting circle on one cardboard circle.
7. Centering fabric pieces over matching cardboard pieces and batting-covered piece, fold edges to wrong side; glue in place.
8. Center and glue chair back piece inside back of chair. Cut a $2^{1}/_{4}$" section from toilet paper tube. Center and glue tube section to inside bottom of chair. Center and glue 3" padded circle on top of toilet paper section. Glue remaining fabric-covered circle on bottom of chair.

LAMP

1. Paint dowel rod and beads as desired.
2. Center and glue $1^{1}/_{4}$" plastic lid over hole in one bead. Aligning holes, glue remaining bead on first bead. Insert one end of dowel into holes in beads; glue in place. Glue mouthwash bottle lid to remaining end of dowel.

BRIDE AND GROOM BOTTLES

*H*ere comes the bride —
and the groom — to dress up
the table at a wedding shower
or rehearsal dinner. You can
create the couple in two
different sizes, one for a
centerpiece and the other for a
place setting. Formal in attire
and a cinch to make from
empty bottles and wooden or
plastic spoons, our perky pair
is a perfect match.

WEDDING COUPLE

CENTERPIECE COUPLE

Recycled items for centerpiece: two champagne bottles and two wooden spoons. *You will also need:* white and black spray paint; flesh-color acrylic paint; paintbrushes; two 12" dia. round doilies; one 6" heart-shaped doily; one 3¹/₄" heart-shaped doily; 15" of ¹/₈"w ribbon; ¹/₂" gold heart-shaped charm; pink, red, and black permanent fine-point markers; curly raffia for hair; tracing paper; white and black construction paper; ¹/₈" hole punch; craft glue; and a hot glue gun.

SMALL COUPLE

Recycled items: two single-serving wine bottles and two plastic spoons. *You will also need:* white and black spray paint; flesh-color acrylic paint; paintbrushes; two 8" dia. round doilies; two 3¹/₄" heart-shaped doilies; 15" of ¹/₈"w ribbon; ³/₈" gold heart-shaped charm; pink, red, and black permanent fine-point markers; curly raffia for hair; tracing paper; white and black construction paper; ¹/₈" hole punch; craft glue; and a hot glue gun.

Allow paint and glue to dry after each application. Use hot glue for all gluing unless otherwise indicated.

BRIDE

1. Spray paint one bottle white. Using flesh-color acrylic paint, paint one spoon.
2. For skirt, fold one round doily in half; glue fold around bottle.
3. For top of dress, position and glue heart-shaped doily (use 6" doily for centerpiece bride) on front of bottle. If desired, glue sides of heart to back of bottle.
4. For face, use markers to draw eyes, eyelashes, eyebrows, and cheeks on spoon. Insert spoon handle into bottle.
5. Tie ribbon into a bow around neck of bottle. Glue charm below bow. For hair,

arrange and glue several lengths of raffia to top of spoon.
6. For veil, fold remaining round doily in half. Fold in half again and cut along folds. Glue points of two doily pieces to back of head. Center and glue remaining heart-shaped doily to back of head. Spot glue veil to back of bottle.

GROOM

1. Spray paint one bottle black. Using flesh-color acrylic paint, paint one spoon.
2. Trace shirt and tie patterns, page 147, onto tracing paper; cut out. Follow solid lines on pattern to cut shirt from white construction paper. Refer to dashed lines on pattern to fold collar. Glue shirt around bottle. From black construction paper, cut tie and punch two holes for buttons. Using craft glue, glue tie and buttons to shirt.
3. For face, use markers to draw eyes, eyebrows, mouth, and cheeks. Insert spoon handle into bottle.
4. For hair, arrange and glue several pieces of curly raffia to top of spoon.

123

JUNK JEWELRY FRAME

*C*lean out the bottom of
your jewelry box and use some
of those throwaway pieces to
create a stylish display for a
special picture. Odd earrings and
abandoned charms make perfect
ornaments for an ordinary wooden
frame. Add some ribbon and an
orphaned spoon, and you'll have a
magnificent treasure!

JUNK JEWELRY FRAME

Recycled items: picture frame, silver-plated
spoon, and costume jewelry.
You will also need: metallic gold paint and
paintbrushes (optional), fine sandpaper,
wired ribbon (we used ¹/₂"w), needlenose
pliers, household cement, and a hot glue
gun.

*Use hot glue for all gluing unless
otherwise indicated.*

1. If desired, paint frame; allow to dry. For
aged look, lightly sand edges of frame.
2. Using pliers, bend spoon to desired
shape. Remove clasps and backs from
jewelry. Using household cement, glue
spoon and jewelry to frame as desired.
3. Tie ribbon into a bow; glue to corner of
frame. Shape ribbon ends along edges of
frame; glue in place.

TAILOR-MADE CIGAR BOXES

*G*reat Father's Day gifts, our cigar boxes are sure to please any Dad or Grandpa! Newsprint stock listings, painted with wood tone spray, cover the tie-trimmed lid of one box. We crafted a padded lid for the top of our wide tie box and affixed a handy hook and loop fastener.

"TIED" CIGAR BOXES

Recycled items: cigar boxes, neckties, assorted buttons, and stock market page from newspaper for Stock Market Box. *You will also need:* a hot glue gun. *For Stock Market Box, you will also need:* wood tone spray and spray adhesive. *For Wide Tie Box, you will also need:* batting, flat trim, and a hook and loop fastener.

Use hot glue for all gluing unless otherwise indicated.

STOCK MARKET BOX
1. Spray stock market page with wood tone spray; allow to dry.
2. Draw around box lid on stock market page. Cut out ¼" inside drawn lines. Spray wrong side of newspaper piece with spray adhesive; center and glue on box lid.
3. Measuring to fit along edges of box lid, cut narrow ends from four ties. With tie points overlapping cut ends of tie pieces, glue tie pieces along edges of newspaper piece.
4. Glue buttons to box as desired.

WIDE TIE BOX
1. Draw around box lid on batting. Cut out batting ¼" inside drawn line. Center and glue batting on box lid.
2. Measure box lid from front to back; add 3". Use determined measurement to cut a piece from wide end of each tie. With pointed end of each tie extending 2" past front edge of lid, arrange and glue tie pieces over batting. Glue remaining edges of tie pieces in place. Cut a piece of flat trim to cover cut ends of ties at back of box; glue in place.
3. Glue one piece of hook and loop fastener to wrong side of middle tie. Glue remaining piece of fastener to front of box under middle tie. Glue buttons to box as desired.

OXFORD STRIPE ACCESSORIES

*O**ur matching dressing table accessories make a stylish statement! Old blue and white oxford shirts are used to cover a lampshade, a tray, and cigar boxes, and ribbon and doilies give the pieces a delicate touch. A padded headband and fashion pin (shown on page 128) let a special lady take this fabulous style with her wherever she goes, and a hand mirror lets her see how lovely she looks wearing the pin-striped pretties!*

OXFORD SHIRT ACCESSORIES

LAMP
Recycled items: oxford shirt, lamp, and a lampshade.
You will also need: spray adhesive, craft glue, and flat trim (optional).

Allow glue to dry after each application.

1. Remove buttons from shirt. Leaving ¹/₂" of shirt fabric along seam of collar, remove collar and buttonhole placket from shirt.
2. Follow *Covering a Lampshade,* page 158, to cover shade with shirt fabric.
3. Glue excess shirt fabric on collar to wrong side. If desired, glue trim to wrong sides of collar and placket with trim extending past edges.

4. Centering placket at front of shade, glue collar around shade. Trimming end of placket as necessary, glue placket to front of shade and end of placket to wrong side of shade.
5. Before gluing a button over each buttonhole, make several stitches through holes on each button.

DECORATIVE TRAY
Recycled items: oxford shirt, cardboard, lace doily, and wooden frame.
You will also need: craft drill, drawer handles, white acrylic paint, paintbrush, frame turn-buttons, self-adhesive felt pads, screwdriver, and spray adhesive.

1. Center handle on each short edge of frame; mark placement for holes. Use craft drill to make holes through frame. Paint frame white; allow to dry.

2. Attach handles to front of frame and turn-buttons to back of frame. Cover screw heads with protective felt pads.

3. Draw around glass on cardboard and wrong side of fabric. Cut out each piece along drawn lines.

4. For insert, use spray adhesive to glue wrong side of fabric to cardboard. Apply spray adhesive to wrong side of doily. Center and glue doily on fabric side of insert.

5. Place glass, then insert in frame. Move frame turn-buttons to hold insert in place.

DOILY BOX

Recycled items: oxford shirt, cigar box, poster board, and a lace doily.
You will also need: 1/2" dia. circle of hook and loop fastener, spray adhesive, and a hot glue gun.

Use hot glue for all gluing unless otherwise indicated.

1. Draw around box lid once on poster board and twice on wrong side of shirt fabric.

2. Cut out poster board 1/4" inside drawn lines. Cut out one fabric piece along drawn line. Apply spray adhesive to wrong side of fabric. Center and glue poster board on wrong side of fabric piece. Fold corners of fabric diagonally over corners of poster board; glue in place. Fold edges of fabric over edges of poster board; glue in place.

3. To cover box lid, cut out remaining fabric piece 1/2" outside drawn lines. Apply spray adhesive to wrong side of fabric. Centering wrong side of fabric on lid, smooth fabric over lid and down hinge side of box. Fold corners of fabric diagonally over corners of lid. Clipping at hinges, fold edges of fabric over edges of lid. Trim fabric even with

side corners.

4. For closure, cut 2" from one point of collar. Center and glue 1/2" of cut edge to wrong side of lid.

5. Follow *Covering a Box,* page 156, to cut fabric from shirt to cover box. Apply spray adhesive to wrong side of fabric and center box on fabric. On hinge side of box, fold fabric edge to wrong side and match folded edge to top edge of box; glue in place. Continue following *Covering a Box* to cover remaining sides of box.

6. Apply spray adhesive to wrong side of doily. Center and apply doily to lid of box. Glue one piece of hook and loop fastener to wrong side of closure and remaining piece to side of box. Glue buttons to closure and box as desired.

7. Center and glue wrong side of covered poster board to inside of lid.

CHARM BOX

Recycled items: oxford shirts, cigar box, poster board, and items to decorate boxes (we used ribbon, lace, and a charm).
You will also need: 1/2"w grosgrain ribbon, spray adhesive, and a hot glue gun.

Use hot glue for all gluing unless otherwise indicated.

1. Follow Steps 1 - 3 of Doily Box to cover box lid. Repeat Step 1 to cut a second piece of fabric from second color shirt. Cut piece in half diagonally and repeat Step 3 to apply one half to lid.

2. Follow Step 5 of Doily Box to cover box.

3. Center and glue wrong side of covered poster board to inside of lid.

4. For tie closure, cut two 12" lengths of ribbon. Glue one end of one ribbon length at center of front edge of lid and one end of remaining ribbon length to center of front side of box. Tie ribbon ends together into a bow.

5. Arrange and glue decorative items to box as desired.

MIRROR

Recycled items: hand mirror, oxford shirt, doily at least ¹/₂" smaller than back of mirror, poster board, and a button.
You will also need: white acrylic paint, paintbrush, batting, ¹/₈"w and ¹/₄"w ribbon, spray adhesive, and a hot glue gun.

Use hot glue for all gluing unless otherwise indicated.

1. Paint handle and back of mirror white, allow to dry.
2. Place doily right side up on poster board. Draw around doily on poster board, remove doily, and mark poster board. Cut out poster board ¹/₄" outside drawn line. Draw around poster board on batting and cut out along drawn line. Matching marked side of poster board to wrong side of shirt fabric, draw around poster board. Cut out fabric 1" outside drawn line.
3. Clip edges of fabric to ¹/₄" from drawn line. Center batting, then poster board on wrong side of fabric. Glue clipped edges of fabric to back of poster board. Glue fabric covered poster board to back of mirror.
4. Apply spray adhesive to wrong side of doily. Center and apply doily to fabric covered poster board. Glue buttons to doily as desired.
5. Tie several lengths of ribbon into a bow around handle.

ROSE PIN

Recycled item: oxford shirt.
You will also need: a pin back and a hot glue gun.

1. Cut a 4" x 21" strip from shirt. Matching wrong sides and long edges, fold strip in half. Using a ¹/₄" seam allowance, baste long edges together.
2. To form center of rose, knot one narrow end of strip. Pull basting thread to gather strip. Knot and trim basting thread. Wind strip loosely around knot, tacking

gathered edge of strip to knot to secure.
3. Continue winding strip around center with bottom edge winding slightly downward and tacking bottom edge in place as you go. At end of strip, fold raw edges ¹/₄" to wrong side and stitch in place.
4. Glue pin back to back of rose.

HEADBAND

Recycled items: oxford shirt, ribbon, flat trim, and a headband.
You will also need: batting and a hot glue gun.

1. Cut a piece of batting to cover outside of headband. Glue batting to headband and trim edges even with edges of headband.

2. Measure headband from end to end; add 1". Measure width of headband at top center; multiply width measurement by two and add ¹/₄". Cut a strip of fabric the determined measurement.
3. Centering headband on wrong side of fabric strip, overlap and glue long edges of fabric to inside of headband. Fold and glue fabric ends to inside of headband.
4. Beginning inside at one end of headband, glue ribbon and trim around headband. Trim and glue ends to inside of headband.
5. Measure along inside of headband; add 1". Cut a length of ribbon the determined measurement. Folding each end ¹/₂" to wrong side, glue wrong side of ribbon over raw edge of fabric on inside of headband.

CHALKBOARD FLOORCLOTH

*W*ith just a few coats of paint and some easy stenciling, a scrap piece of vinyl flooring becomes a cheerful floorcloth for kids. This chalkboard-look project includes a special feature — kids can really write on it!

CHALKBOARD FLOORCLOTH

Recycled item: piece of vinyl flooring (we used a 24" x 36" piece of vinyl).

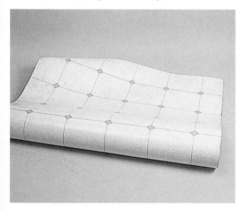

You will also need: flat black spray paint, removable tape, white acrylic paint, ³/₈"w and ⁵/₈"w flat-edge paintbrushes, alphabet and number stencils, desired colors of acrylic paint, sponge, and spray matte sealer.

Allow paint and sealer to dry after each application.

1. Apply two coats of black paint to the wrong side of vinyl flooring piece.
2. For inner border, place a strip of tape 4¹/₂" inside edge around all sides of flooring piece. Place a second strip of tape ¹/₂" outside first strip around all sides. Use ³/₈"w paintbrush to paint evenly spaced white marks between strips of tape.

3. For outer border, place a strip of tape ⁵/₈" inside all edges of flooring piece. Use ⁵/₈"w paintbrush to paint evenly spaced white marks along outer edge.
4. Remove tape. Use stencils, sponge, and desired color paint to paint alphabet and numbers inside borders.
5. Spray entire surface with sealer.

PATTERNS

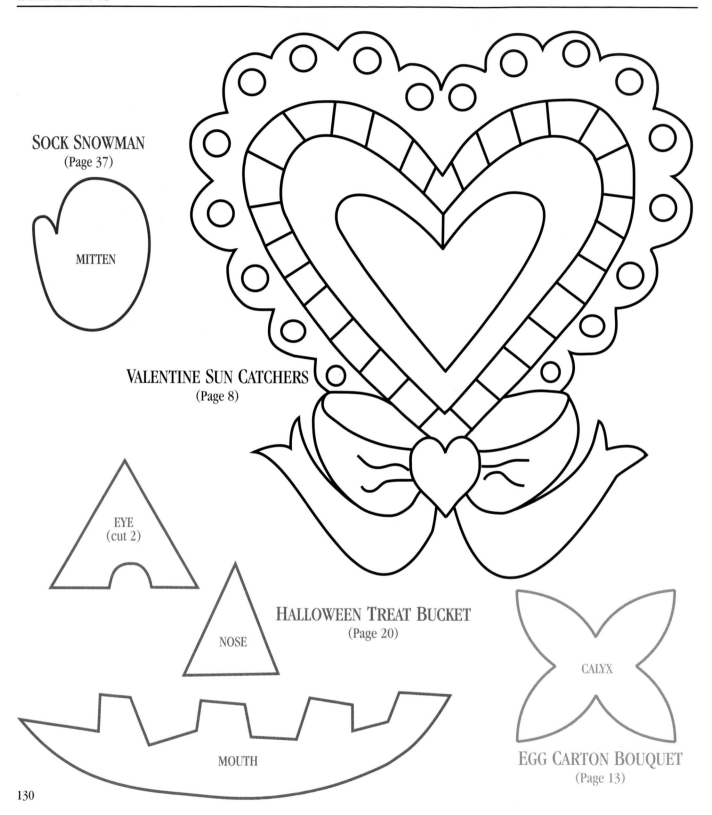

SOCK SNOWMAN
(Page 37)

MITTEN

VALENTINE SUN CATCHERS
(Page 8)

EYE
(cut 2)

NOSE

HALLOWEEN TREAT BUCKET
(Page 20)

CALYX

MOUTH

EGG CARTON BOUQUET
(Page 13)

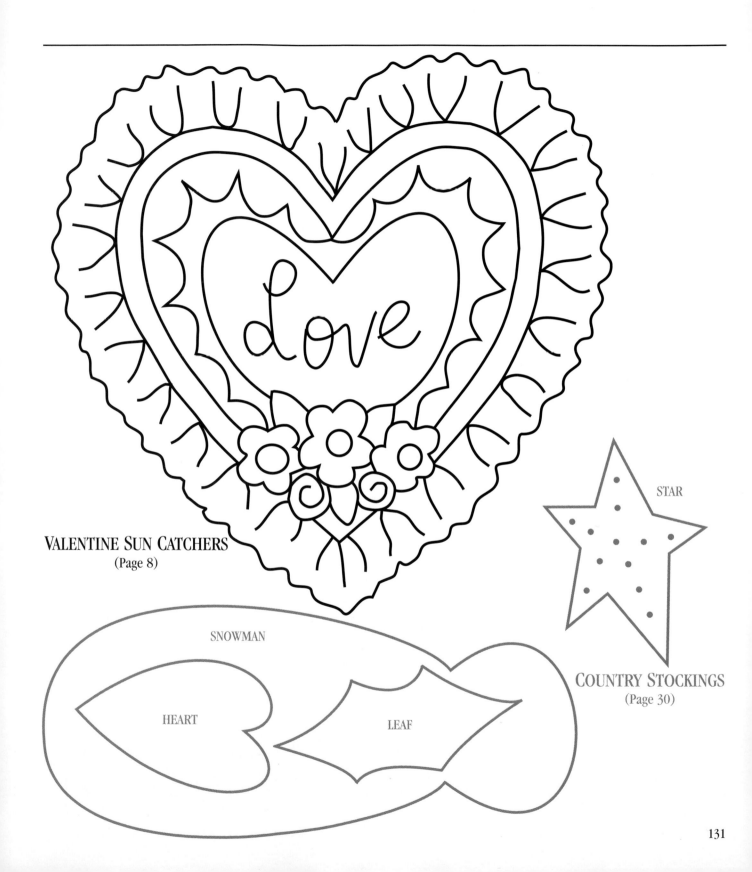

VALENTINE SUN CATCHERS
(Page 8)

STAR

COUNTRY STOCKINGS
(Page 30)

SNOWMAN

HEART

LEAF

PATTERNS (continued)

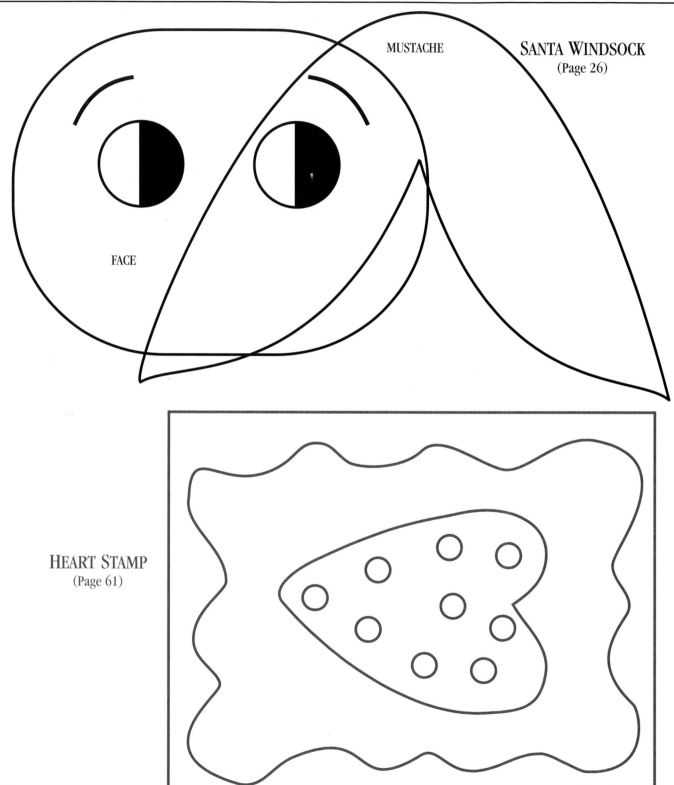

MUSTACHE

SANTA WINDSOCK
(Page 26)

FACE

HEART STAMP
(Page 61)

VALENTINE SHIRT
(Page 9)

NOSE UNCLE SAM
(Page 14)

WING

HALLOWEEN TREAT BOXES
(Page 21)

EAR

PATTERNS (continued)

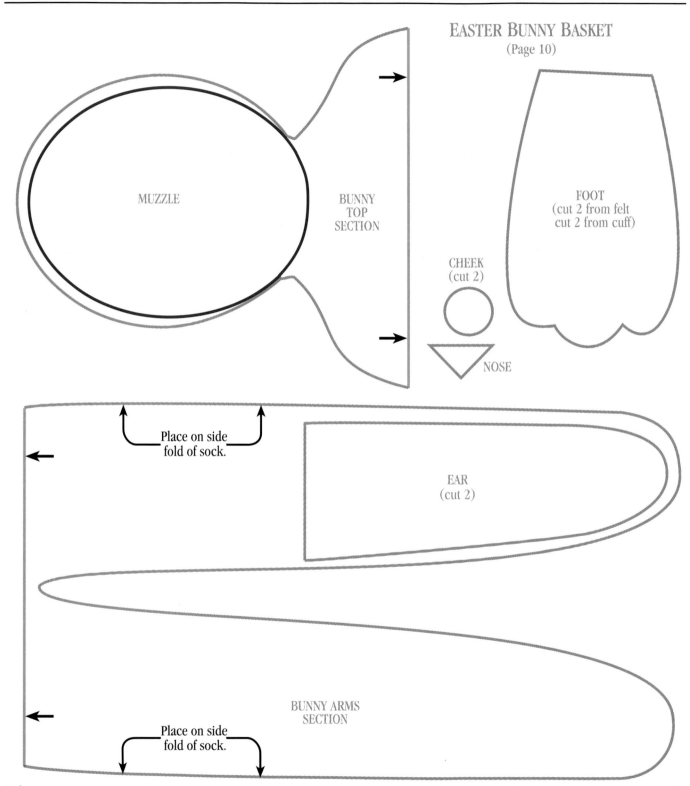

EASTER BUNNY BASKET
(Page 10)

MUZZLE

BUNNY
TOP
SECTION

CHEEK
(cut 2)

NOSE

FOOT
(cut 2 from felt
cut 2 from cuff)

Place on side
fold of sock.

EAR
(cut 2)

BUNNY ARMS
SECTION

Place on side
fold of sock.

EASTER BUNNY BASKET
(Page 10)

Hoppy Easter!

TIN-PUNCHED ORNAMENTS
(Page 25)

LIGHT BULB ORNAMENTS
(Page 24)

BOW TIE

TIE CENTER

EAR
(cut 2)

PATTERNS (continued)

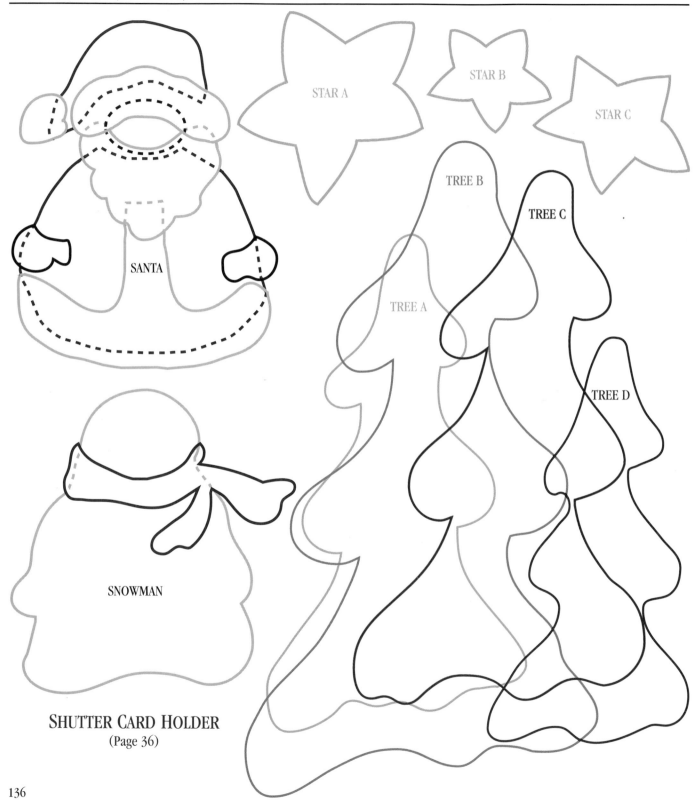

STAR A

STAR B

STAR C

SANTA

TREE B

TREE C

TREE A

TREE D

SNOWMAN

SHUTTER CARD HOLDER
(Page 36)

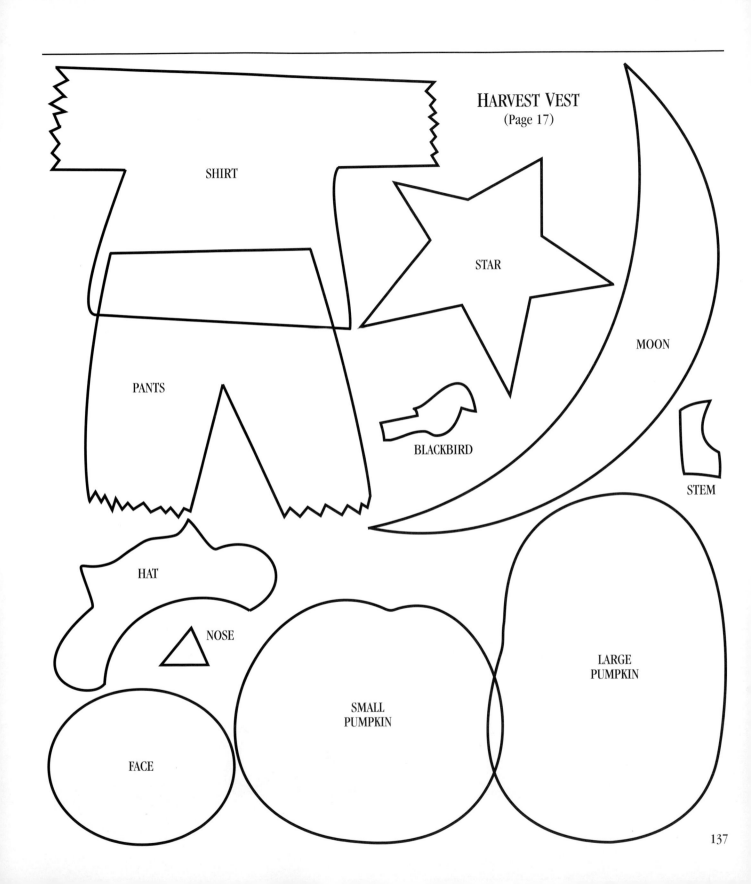

HARVEST VEST
(Page 17)

SHIRT

STAR

MOON

PANTS

BLACKBIRD

STEM

HAT

NOSE

LARGE
PUMPKIN

SMALL
PUMPKIN

FACE

137

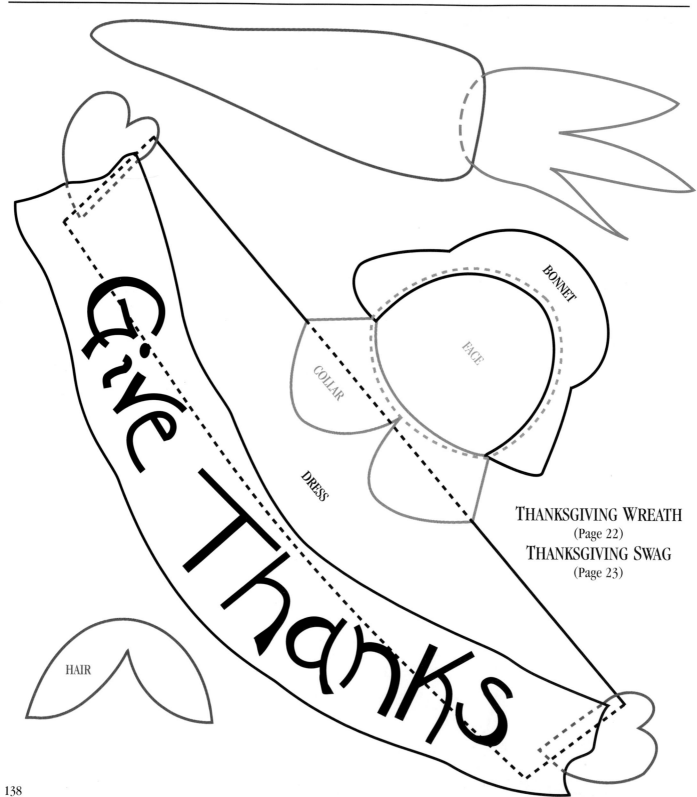

Give Thanks

BONNET

FACE

COLLAR

DRESS

HAIR

THANKSGIVING WREATH
(Page 22)
THANKSGIVING SWAG
(Page 23)

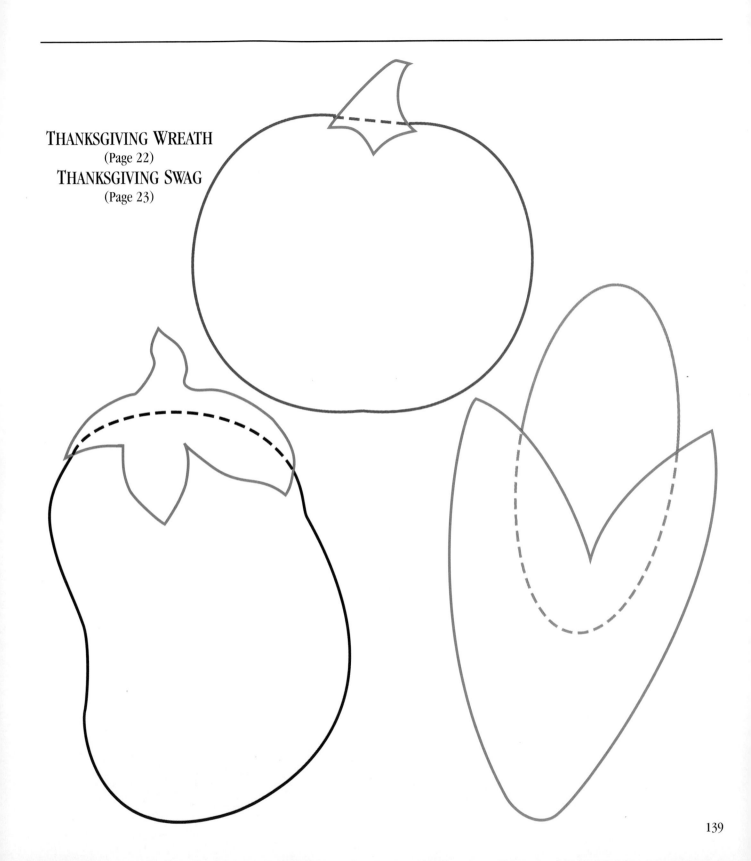

THANKSGIVING WREATH
(Page 22)
THANKSGIVING SWAG
(Page 23)

139

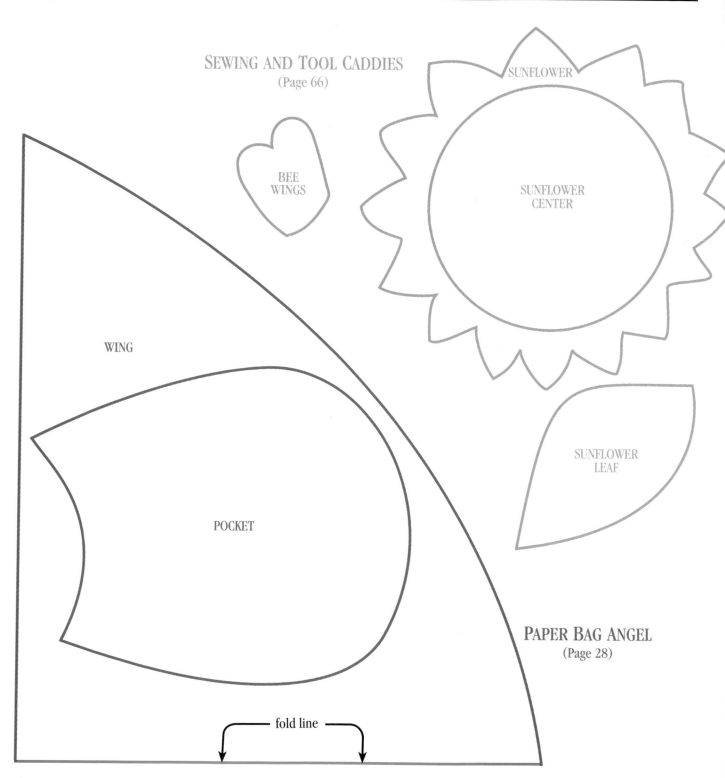

SEWING AND TOOL CADDIES
(Page 66)

BEE
WINGS

SUNFLOWER

SUNFLOWER
CENTER

WING

SUNFLOWER
LEAF

POCKET

PAPER BAG ANGEL
(Page 28)

fold line

FOAM TRAY ACCESSORIES
(Page 44)

MEDALLION

FEATHER

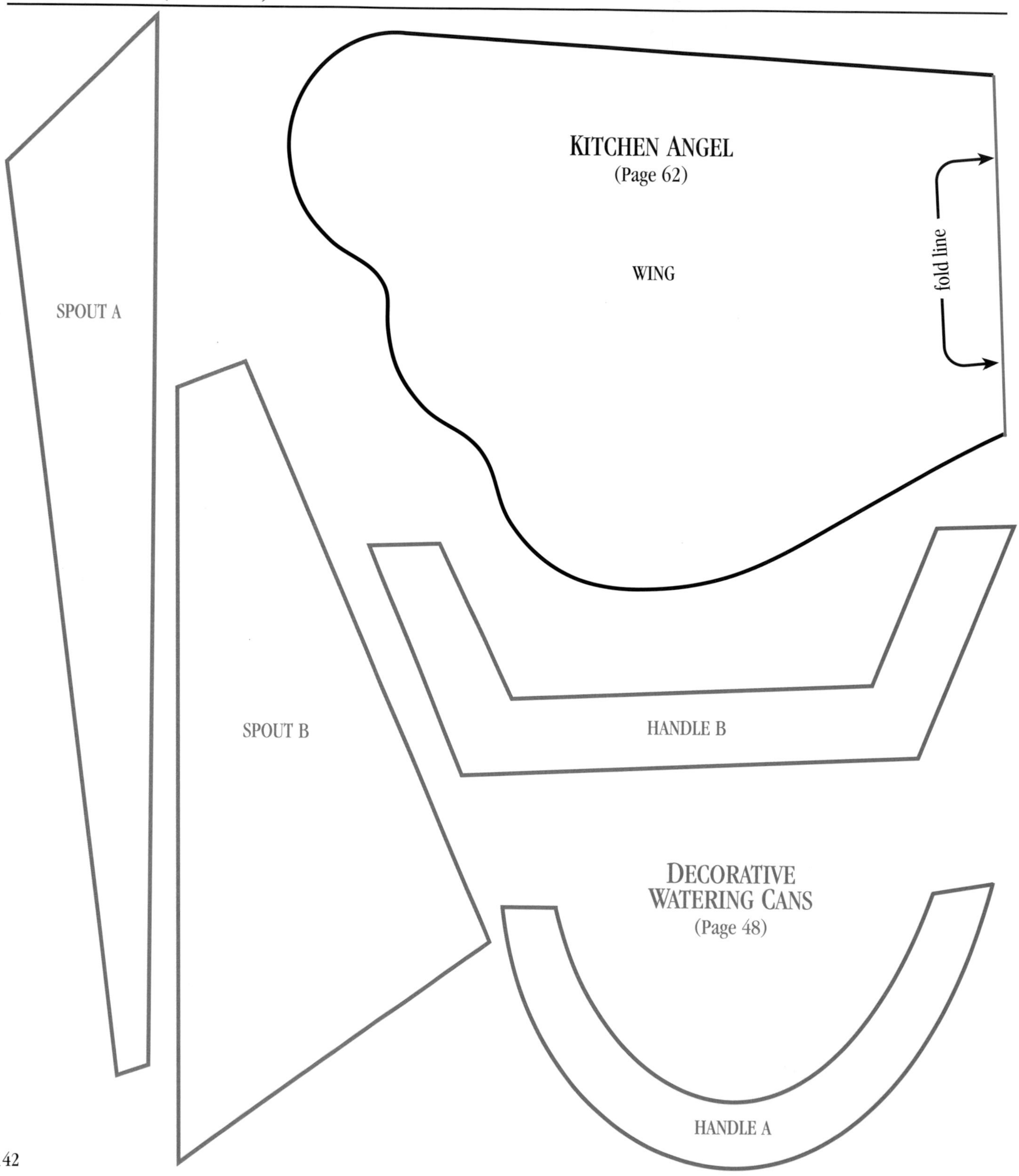

SPOUT A

KITCHEN ANGEL
(Page 62)

WING

fold line

SPOUT B

HANDLE B

DECORATIVE
WATERING CANS
(Page 48)

HANDLE A

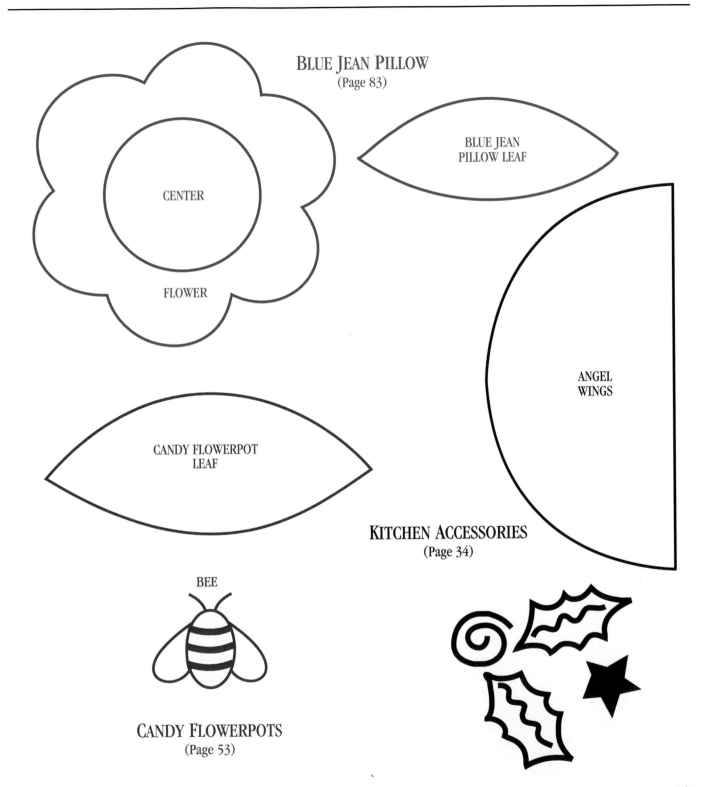

BLUE JEAN PILLOW
(Page 83)

BLUE JEAN
PILLOW LEAF

CENTER

FLOWER

ANGEL
WINGS

CANDY FLOWERPOT
LEAF

KITCHEN ACCESSORIES
(Page 34)

BEE

CANDY FLOWERPOTS
(Page 53)

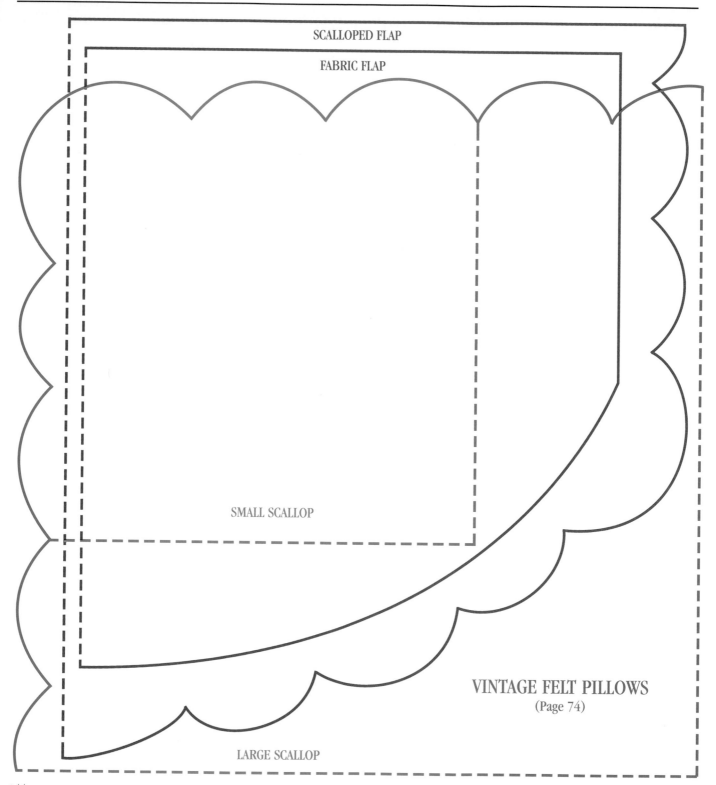

SCALLOPED FLAP

FABRIC FLAP

SMALL SCALLOP

LARGE SCALLOP

VINTAGE FELT PILLOWS
(Page 74)

SURPRISE!

HAPPY BIRTHDAY TO YOU!

GIFT IN A CAN
(Page 52)

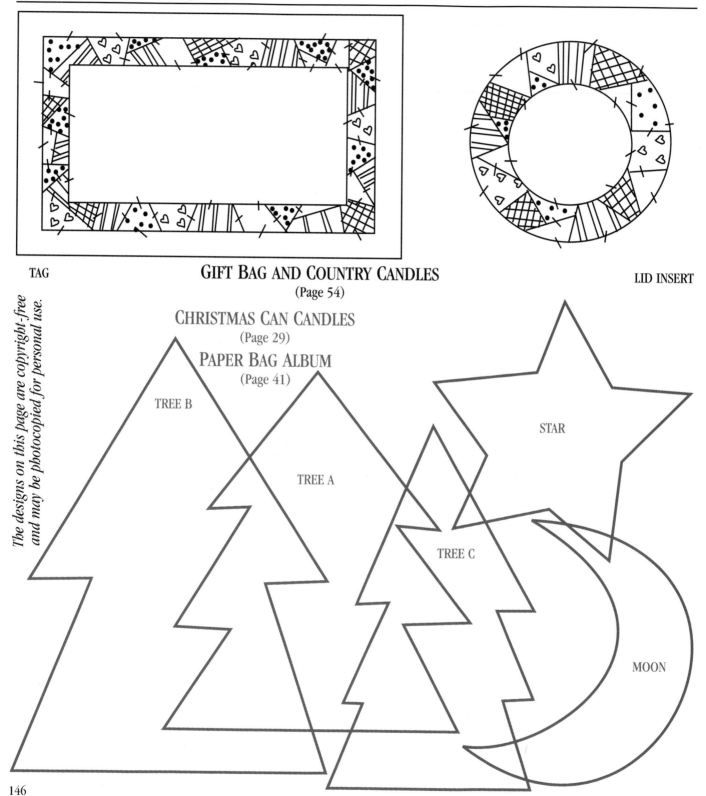

TAG

GIFT BAG AND COUNTRY CANDLES
(Page 54)

LID INSERT

CHRISTMAS CAN CANDLES
(Page 29)

PAPER BAG ALBUM
(Page 41)

TREE B

TREE A

TREE C

STAR

MOON

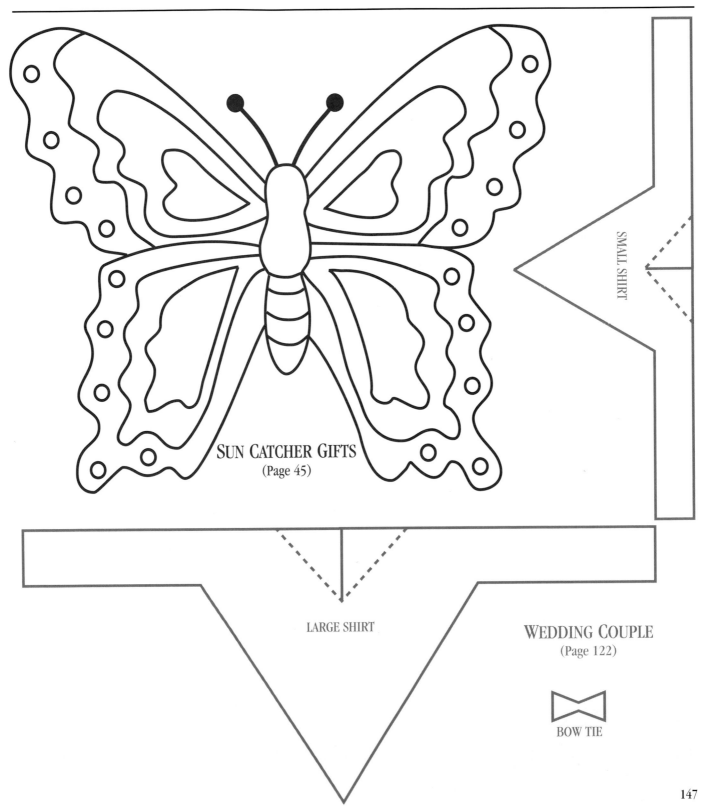

SUN CATCHER GIFTS
(Page 45)

LARGE SHIRT

WEDDING COUPLE
(Page 122)

BOW TIE

SUN CATCHER GIFTS
(Page 45)

CIRCUS PARTY TRAIN
(Page 114)

HAT

LEAF

PICNIC BASKET
(Page 104)

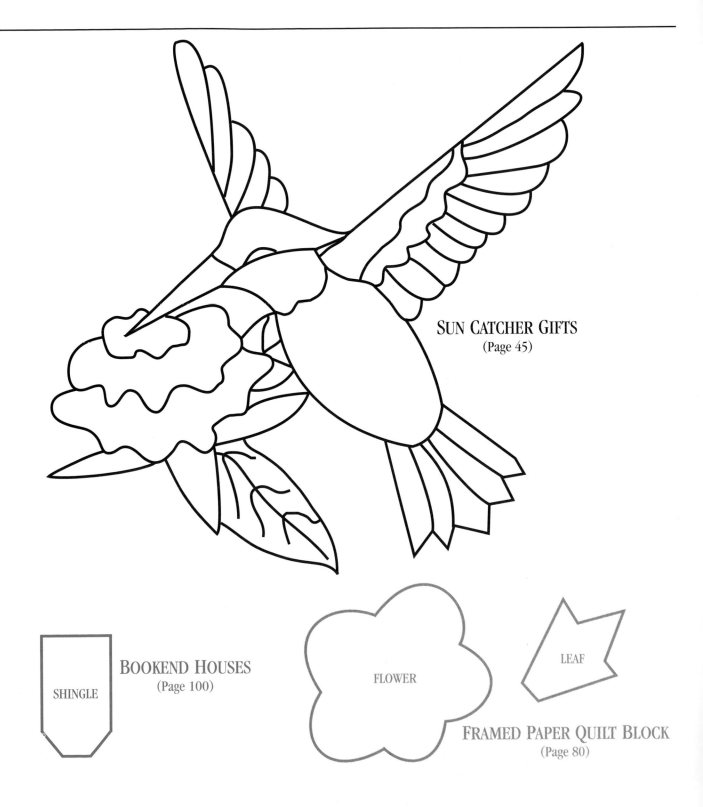

SUN CATCHER GIFTS
(Page 45)

SHINGLE

BOOKEND HOUSES
(Page 100)

FLOWER

LEAF

FRAMED PAPER QUILT BLOCK
(Page 80)

BABY BIBS
(Page 65)

fold line

CHAIR

fold line

DOLL FURNITURE
(Page 120)

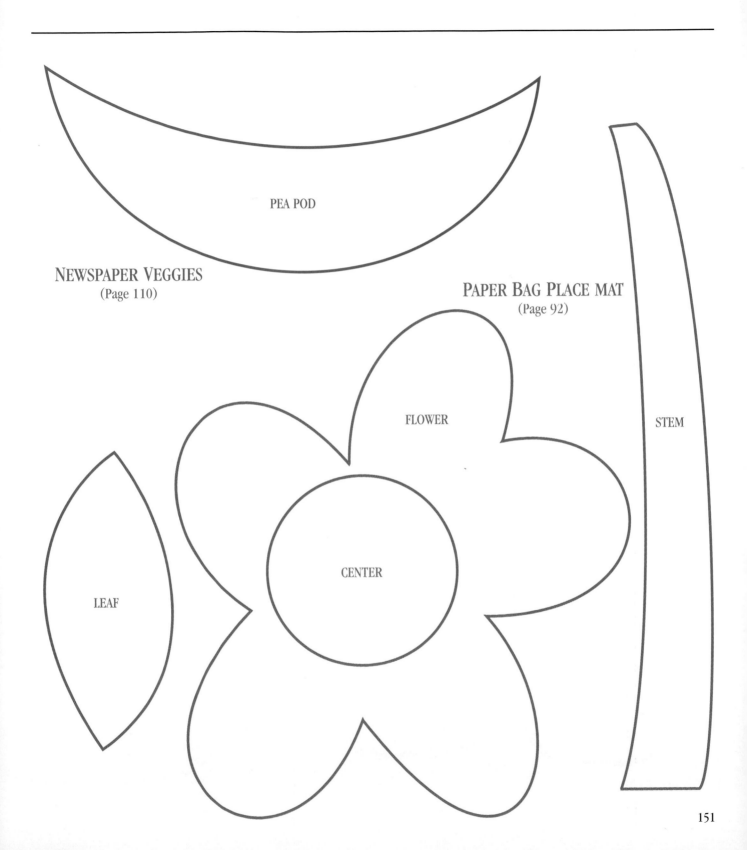

PEA POD

NEWSPAPER VEGGIES
(Page 110)

PAPER BAG PLACE MAT
(Page 92)

STEM

FLOWER

LEAF

CENTER

PATTERNS (continued)

*The designs on this page are copyright-free
and may be photocopied for personal use.*

NURSERY LAMP
(Page 89)

PLASTIC BAG KEEPER
(Page 117)

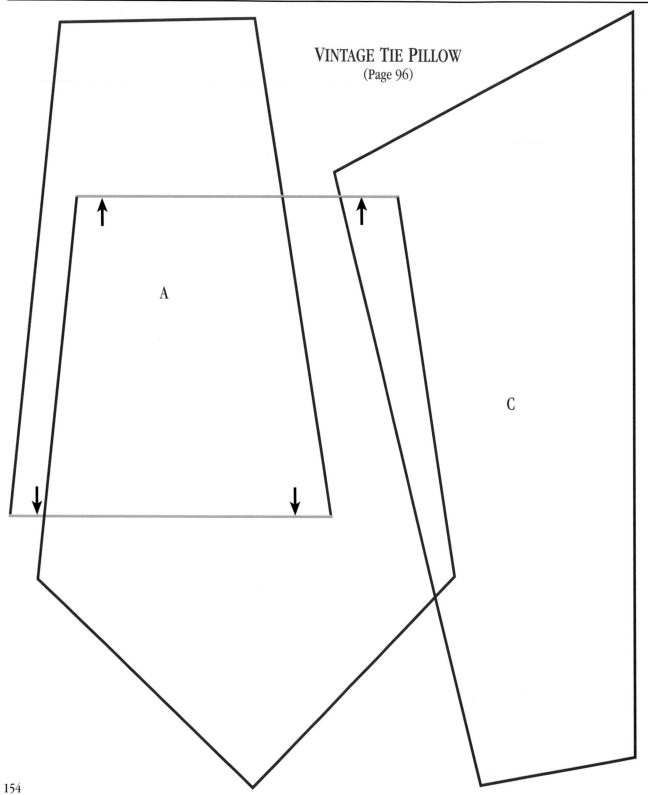

VINTAGE TIE PILLOW
(Page 96)

A

C

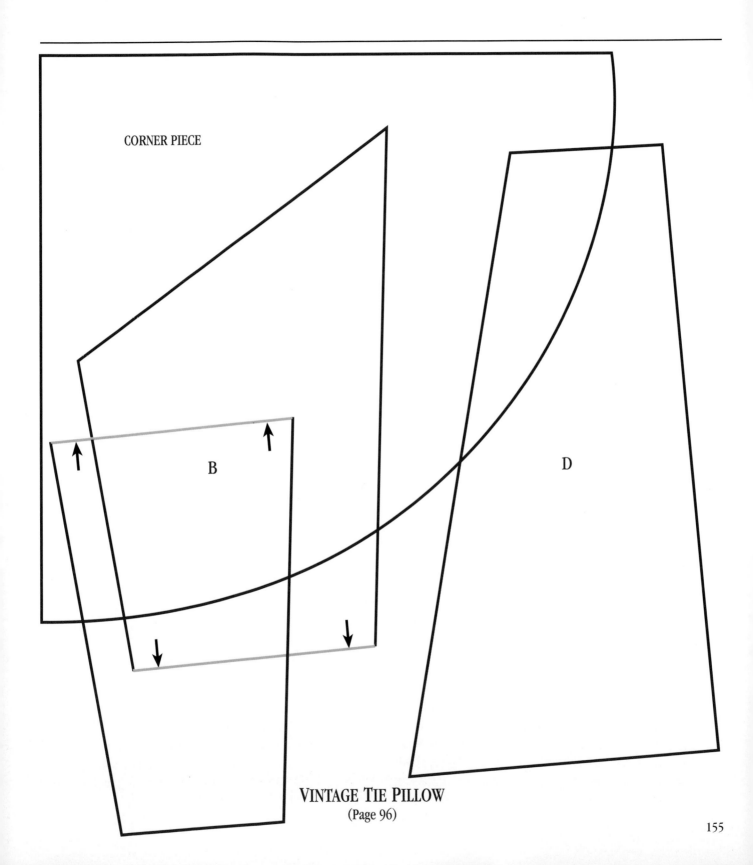

CORNER PIECE

B

D

VINTAGE TIE PILLOW
(Page 96)

155

GENERAL INSTRUCTIONS

ADHESIVES AND GLUES

GLUE	USES (★ — recommended, ■ — can also be used)							DRYING INFORMATION
	paper	fabric	floral	ceramic	wood	metal	stencils	
craft glue	★	■	■					dry flat *or* secure items with clothespins or straight pins until dry
thick craft glue	■	■	■					items may need support until dry
fabric glue	■	★						dry flat or secure items with clothespins or straight pins until dry
hot glue	■	■	★			■		hold in place until set
household cement				★		★		secure items until set
spray adhesive	■	■					■	apply to one or both surfaces and press together
wood glue					★			items must be nailed, screwed, or clamped together until set
stencil adhesive							★	apply to back of stencil and press onto item to be stenciled

COFFEE DYEING

1. Dissolve two tablespoons instant coffee in two cups hot water; allow to cool.
2. Soak fabric pieces in coffee several minutes. Remove from coffee and allow to dry; press.

COVERING A BOX

To cover a box with fabric, substitute fabric when paper is indicated.

1. Cut a piece of paper large enough to cover box. Center box on wrong side of paper and draw around box.
2. Use ruler to draw lines ¹/₂" outside drawn lines, extending lines to edges of paper. Draw diagonal lines from intersections of outer lines to corners of original lines.

3. Cut away corners of paper and clip along diagonal lines (Fig. 1).

Fig. 1

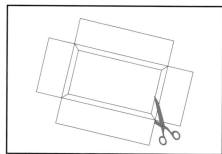

4. Apply spray adhesive to wrong side of paper.
5. Center box on paper, matching box to original drawn lines; smooth paper on bottom of box.
6. To cover front and back of box, smooth paper onto front and back sides of box.

Smooth excess paper around corners onto adjacent sides. Smooth paper to inside of box, clipping as necessary (Fig. 2).

Fig. 2

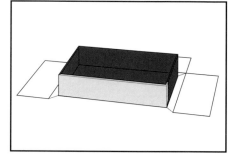

7. To cover each end, smooth paper onto end of box. Use craft knife and ruler to trim excess paper even with corners. Smooth paper to inside of box.

MAKING PATTERNS

For a more durable pattern, use a permanent pen to trace pattern onto stencil plastic.

WHOLE PATTERN
Place tracing paper over pattern and trace pattern; cut out.

HALF PATTERN
Indicated by blue line on pattern.

1. Fold tracing paper in half and match fold to blue line of pattern.
2. Trace pattern half; turn folded paper over and draw over traced lines on remaining side of paper.
3. Unfold paper and cut out pattern.

SECTIONED PATTERN
Indicated by grey line on pattern.

1. Trace one pattern section.
2. Matching grey lines and arrows, trace remaining section to complete pattern; cut out.

CUTTING A FABRIC CIRCLE

1. Cut a square of fabric the size indicated in project instructions.
2. Matching right sides, fold fabric square in half from top to bottom and again from left to right.
3. Tie one end of a length of string to a pencil. Measuring from pencil, insert a thumbtack through string at length indicated in project instructions. Insert thumbtack through folded corner of fabric. Holding tack in place and keeping string taut, mark cutting line (Fig 1).

Fig. 1

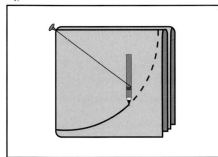

4. For additional cutting lines, repeat Step 3.
5. Cut along drawn lines through all fabric layers.

PREPARING AN ITEM FOR PAINTING OR DECOUPAGE

Caution: Work in a well-ventilated area when using cleaners. Wear protective gloves and clothing as needed. Cover work area with plastic or newspaper.

You will need: household cleaner, sponge or scouring pad, and a soft damp cloth.
You may also need: fine grit sandpaper or steel wool, tack cloth, masking tape, and spray primer.

1. Use cleaner and either sponge or scouring pad to clean item. Remove cleaner with damp cloth; allow to dry. If rust is present, lightly sand or rub with steel wool to remove. Wipe clean with tack cloth; allow to dry.
2. (*Note:* Unfinished metal items will need a coat of primer before applying base coat.) Follow project instructions to apply finishes.

DECOUPAGE

To make decoupage glue, mix one part water with one part craft glue.

1. Cut desired motifs from fabric or paper.
2. Apply decoupage glue to wrong sides of motifs.
3. Arrange motifs on project as desired, overlapping as necessary. Smooth in place and allow to dry.
4. Allowing to dry after each application, spray project with two to three coats of varnish.

DIMENSIONAL PAINT

Before painting on project, practice painting on scrap fabric or paper.

1. To keep paint flowing smoothly, turn bottle upside down and allow paint to fill tip of bottle before each use.
2. Clean tip often with a paper towel.
3. If tip becomes clogged, insert a straight pin into tip opening.
4. When painting lines or painting over appliqués, keep bottle tip in contact with surface of project, applying a thick line of paint centered over drawn line or raw edge of appliqué.

5. To correct a mistake, use a paring knife to gently scrape excess paint from project before it dries. Carefully remove stain with non-acetone nail polish remover. A mistake may also be camouflaged by incorporating the mistake into the design.
6. Lay project flat for 24 hours to ensure that paint is set.

MAKING APPLIQUÉS

White or light-colored fabrics may need to be lined with fusible interfacing before applying paper-backed fusible web to prevent darker fabrics from showing through.

To make reverse appliqué pieces, trace pattern onto tracing paper; turn traced pattern over and continue to follow all steps using reversed pattern.

1. Use a pencil to trace pattern onto paper side of web as many times as indicated in project instructions for a single fabric. Repeat for additional patterns and fabrics.
2. Follow manufacturer's instructions to fuse traced patterns to wrong side of fabrics. Do not remove paper backing.
3. Cut out appliqué pieces along traced lines. Remove paper backing.
4. Arrange appliqués, web side down, on project, overlapping as necessary. Appliqués can be temporarily held in place by touching appliqués with tip of iron. If appliqués are not in desired position, lift and reposition.
5. Fuse appliqués in place.

MACHINE APPLIQUÉ

Unless otherwise indicated in project instructions, set sewing machine for a medium-width zigzag stitch with a short stitch length. When using nylon or metallic thread for appliqué, use regular thread in bobbin.

1. Pin or baste a piece of stabilizer slightly larger than design to wrong side of background fabric under design.
2. Beginning on straight edge of appliqué if possible, position project under presser foot so that most of stitching will be on appliqué piece. Hold upper thread toward you and sew two or three stitches over thread to prevent raveling. Stitch over all exposed raw edges of appliqué and along detail lines as indicated in project instructions.
3. When stitching is complete, remove stabilizer. Pull loose threads to wrong side of fabric; knot and trim ends.

MAKING A FABRIC YO-YO

1. Use compass to draw a circle on tracing paper the diameter indicated in project instructions. Use pattern to cut out fabric circle.
2. Turn raw edge of circle 1/4" to wrong side.
3. Using a double strand of thread, work a small *Running Stitch,* page 159, along turned edge.
4. Pull ends of thread to tightly gather circle; knot thread.
5. Flatten circle with gathers at center.

MAKING A BOW

1. Leaving one ribbon end free for desired length streamer, hold ribbon between index finger and thumb. Make a loop on each side of thumb (Fig. 1).

Fig. 1

2. Continue making loops on each side of thumb for desired number of loops (Fig. 2).

Fig. 2

3. To secure bow, tightly tie a length of ribbon or twist a length of wire around center of bow.

WORKING WITH WAX

MELTING WAX

Caution: Do not melt wax over an open flame or in a pan placed directly on burner.

1. Cover work area with newspaper.
2. Heat 1" of water in a saucepan to boiling. Add water as necessary.
3. Place wax in a large can. If pouring wax, pinch top rim of can to form a spout. If dipping candles, use a can 2" taller than height of candle to be dipped.
4. To melt wax, place can in boiling water, reduce heat to simmer. If desired, melt pieces of crayon in wax for color. Use a craft stick to stir if necessary.

SETTING WICKS AND POURING WAX

1. Cut a length of wax-coated wick 1" longer than depth of candle container.
2. Using an oven mitt, carefully pour wax into container.
3. Allow wax to harden slightly and insert wick at center of candle. Allow wax to harden completely.

DIPPING CANDLES

1. Holding candle by wick, carefully dip candle into wax; allow to harden slightly. Repeat for additional coats of wax.
2. After final dipping, place candles away from heat and allow to harden completely.

COVERING A LAMPSHADE

1. To make pattern, find seamline of lampshade. If shade does not have a seamline, draw a vertical line from top edge to bottom edge of shade.
2. Centering tissue paper edge on shade seamline; tape in place. Wrap paper around shade extending one inch past seamline; tape to secure (Fig. 1).

Fig. 1

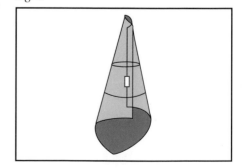

3. Trace along top and bottom edges of shade. Draw a vertical line from top edge to bottom edge of shade 1" past seamline. Remove paper; cut along drawn lines.

4. Use pattern to cut cover from desired fabric or paper.

5. Fold one straight edge of covering 1/2" to wrong side; press.

6. Matching unpressed straight edge of covering to seamline, use spray adhesive to apply covering to shade. Use glue to secure pressed edge.

SPONGE PAINTING

NATURAL SPONGE

1. Dampen sponge with water.

2. Dip dampened sponge into paint; blot on paper towel to remove excess paint.

3. Use a light stamping motion to paint item.

COMPRESSED SPONGE

1. Cut sponge according to project instructions.

2. Expand sponge in water. Squeeze excess water from sponge.

3. Dip dampened sponge into paint; blot on paper towel to remove excess paint.

4. Using even pressure, carefully press paint side of sponge on project.

EMBROIDERY STITCHES

STRAIGHT STITCH

Bring needle up at 1 and go down at 2 (Fig. 1). Length of stitches may be varied as desired.

Fig. 1

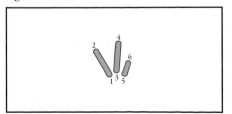

BLANKET STITCH

Bring needle up at 1; keeping thread below point of needle, go down at 2 and come up at 3 (Fig. 2a). Continue working as shown in Fig. 2b.

Fig. 2a

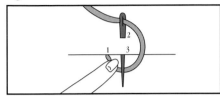

Fig. 2b

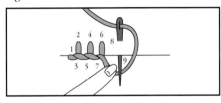

COUCHING STITCH

Thread first needle with desired number of strands of floss to be couched. Thread a second needle with stitching floss. Bring first needle up through fabric. Using second needle, bring needle up at 1 and down at 2 to secure floss (Fig. 3). Repeat to secure floss along desired line.

Fig. 3

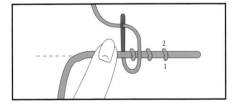

CROSS STITCH

Bring needle up at 1 and go down at 2. Come up at 3 and go down at 4 (Fig. 4).

Fig. 4

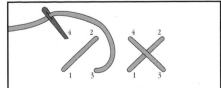

RUNNING STITCH

Make a series of straight stitches with stitch length equal to the space between stitches (Fig. 5).

Fig. 5

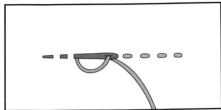

SATIN STITCH

Bring needle up at odd numbers and go down at even numbers with the stitches touching but not overlapping (Fig. 6).

Fig. 6

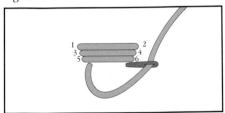

FRENCH KNOT

Bring needle up at 1. Wrap floss once around needle and insert needle at 2, holding floss with non-stitching fingers (Fig. 7). Tighten knot as close to fabric as possible while pulling needle back through fabric. For larger knot, use more strands of floss; wrap only once.

Fig. 7

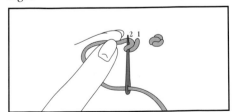

CREDITS

We want to extend a warm *thank you* to the generous people who allowed us to photograph our projects in their homes: Joan Adams, Nancy Appleton, Barbara Barré, Laney and Mary Jane Briggs, Richard and Lange Cheek, Pam Skiles, and Gail Wilcox.

To Magna IV Color Imaging of Little Rock, Arkansas, we say thank you for the superb color reproduction and excellent pre-press preparation.

We especially want to thank photographers David Hale, Jr., Mark Mathews, Larry Pennington, Karen Shirey, and Ken West of Peerless Photography, and Jerry R. Davis of Jerry Davis Photography, all of Little Rock, Arkansas, for their time, patience, and excellent work.

To the talented people who helped in the creation of the following projects in this book, we extend a special word of thanks:

- *Vintage Linen Gifts,* page 42: Julie T. Wilson
- *Vintage Tie Pillow,* page 96: Lucille K. Smith